Breeding for success
in the exhibition
NETHERLAND
DWARF

by GARY HODSON

Breeding For Success In The Exhibition Netherland Dwarf
By Gary Hodson

1st edition 2019

ISBN 978-1-898015-33-8

Typeset in Adobe Garamond

Published and printed in Great Britain
by Printing for Pleasure, Ipswich, Suffolk IP8 3QE
© 2019

Other rabbit breed titles are available at
www.furandfeather.co.uk

This book is dedicated to everyone who breeds and shows Netherland Dwarf rabbits, but in particular those who have held positions in any of the area dwarf clubs and of course the National Netherland Dwarf Rabbit Club, without whom the exhibition Netherland Dwarf wouldn't be where it is today.

My particular thanks to Allan Rudd, my biology teacher, who not only inspired my career as a biology teacher but gave me my first dwarfs, the late Alf Bottomley, my mentor in the early days, the late John Beck, so knowledgeable about all aspects of breeding and exhibiting dwarfs and Jan Lucas, the best judge I have the pleasure of showing under. I would like to thank my wife Deb who has been my partner since 1983 sharing this wonderful hobby, to Simon for his stunning photographs and all the great friends that I have met along the way, Nigel Atkinson, Simon Beynon, Kevin Farnsworth, and Trevor Hoole; friends for life because of this great hobby. I have learnt so much from this group, so any mistakes in this book are their fault.

Preface

I had kept livestock all my life but it was whilst studying for my A levels in 1978 that I was introduced to the world of exhibition dwarfs. Completing my A levels in 1980 gave me the chance to devote more time to take the hobby seriously, and it was then that I met Alf Bottomley, secretary of Bradford Metro Fur Fanciers, and before long was heavily involved in running shows. So my association with Fur and Feather began, writing club notes for Bradford Metro, and subsequently the Northern Area Netherland Club for 25 years and latterly the National Netherland Dwarf Rabbit Club. This evolved into show write ups and a series of articles for the club yearbooks. The National Dwarf Club celebrates its 70th anniversary in 2019 and as I was starting to think about putting together the history of the club for the Club stand at Bradford and London Shows I was asked by the editor of Fur and Feather if I would be willing to write an updated version of Phil Birch's excellent book of 1997 on exhibition Netherland dwarfs to demonstrate their evolution over 70 years.

Netherland dwarfs are freaks of Nature and as a result do not breed as true as many other breeds. I am convinced that is the main reason why many people's experiences of breeding exhibition dwarfs are short lived. My aim has always been to help dwarfs fanciers establish a line of exhibition dwarfs that they could call their own and enjoy the success that comes with breeding and showing Netherland dwarfs.

Gary Hodson

The importance of joining a club

Exhibiting your dwarfs should be a social event so the best way to meet like minded people is to get involved with your local clubs; there is always plenty to do on show days. Equally as important is that you join the National Netherland Dwarf Rabbit Club and your local area dwarf club and make every effort to attend their shows. This is where you will see the best dwarfs exhibited throughout the UK and you can assess your stock against what is on show and meet and get advice from the most experienced breeders. Full details of all clubs and shows can be found in the Fur and Feather.

Chapter 1

In the Beginning

There are many different ways that exhibitors begin to show netherland dwarfs; many start off with a pet, usually junior exhibitors, and then progress into the world of showing after obtaining stock from a breeder local to them. Other junior exhibitors are lucky enough to be born into a family of rabbit breeders and so are off to a flying start. The main problem today is that children have so many other hobbies that fewer and fewer have any form of livestock.

No matter what age you are, getting initial stock to breed from can be difficult, and it is becoming more and more difficult with the legislation around data protection. In the past, the advice was to contact the British Rabbit Council or National Netherland Dwarf Rabbit Club or area dwarf club Secretary for details of local breeders. Nowadays it is not possible to pass on such information without the express permission of the breeder. The best advice that we can give is to visit a show that is entertaining a dwarf stock show, this ensures that there will be lots of dwarf breeders and exhibitors, and a range of colours to choose from.

The key to success is patience; you shouldn't buy the first dwarfs that you see. Introduce yourself to the breeders and get chatting about the hobby. Ask if you can visit them at home to see their stock and hopefully you will make a lifelong friend in the hobby. After doing your research into the colours that you prefer, the full list of available colours can be found in the National Netherland Dwarf Rabbit Club yearbook and photos of all the show winners can be found on the website. If you contact the secretaries, details on the website, they may have spare yearbooks from previous years that they would let you have in return for a contribution towards the postage costs. Not only will you find an illustrated breed standard with all the colours, you will very quickly be able to identify the successful exhibitors with each colour.

After doing your research, it is time to look into the purchase of your foundation stock. The best advice at this point is to stick to one colour at first, or at the most two compatible colours. The breeder can advise you on which colours can be successfully bred together. The cost varies tremendously and it is up to the breeder to set his or her own price, but remember the old adage, "you get what you pay for." Like most small livestock hobbies, the price of stock has remained dormant for many years, there are many instances of stock being sold for the same price now as 20 years ago. I would advise trying to buy a trio (1 buck and two does) or two pairs from the breeder. If you buy just a pair, the buck and the doe may just not "click" when bred together, and breed nothing but pet quality dwarfs. Remember that most breeders do not breed all year round, they breed for certain shows so will only have dwarfs available at certain times of the year. A popular time to breed youngsters is April as they will be the correct age to be successful at the Young Stock Shows in September, i.e. 5 months old. So breeders may well have surplus to spare in the early summer months up to the end of September.

Once you have your stock it is time to start breeding. Take the breeders advice on what to breed to what if you have more than 1 buck. Don't be too disheartened if the does lose their first litter, especially maiden does (those that haven't had a litter before). Lots of breeders have different opinions on when to remate the does that lose litters, so listen to the advice and then do what you are comfortable with. Hopefully this won't be the case and you will have litters of youngsters to pick the best from. Most exhibitors check the nest after they are born, and then leave the doe to bring up the litter in peace. The young can be assessed at 4 weeks, I would ask the advice of the person that you bought the stock from as they know how their strain develops. In our case, we make an initial judgement at 4 weeks and re-assess at 6 weeks when the youngsters are weaned. At this point they are rung, and no matter how nice it looks, if we cannot get a ring on at 6 weeks, it will be too big. There is space in the stud for these 'bigger' dwarfs, which will be addressed later in the book.

Once your numbers start to grow, you will need to develop a system to breed to. Whilst some breeders don't follow a system, the more consistent and successful breeders do. There are several strategies employed by the most successful exhibitors, all of which are based around selective breeding. This involves breeding together related individuals to fix desirable characteristics into your stud. However, this isn't as straightforward as it appears. Whilst you can increase the numbers of alleles (specific genes) for desirable characteristics, you can just as easily increase the number of alleles for recessive undesirable characteristics. This is where critical analysis of your stock is so important. It is no use breeding a dwarf which excels on head and body if it has thin bowed ears. Study the standard carefully and compare your youngsters to it. At this point it definitely helps to get a second opinion. Like many successful studs we breed grandfather to granddaughter. Obviously the strategy will depend on the stock that you have, and no matter what system you use, you should never bred together two dwarfs with the same fault.

Netherland dwarfs have a reputation for being difficult to breed, and whilst this is true to some extent, there is a simple strategy that will improve your success rate. Like all characteristics, being a good mother is genetic, so just like your selection of dwarfs for a good head, good body shape, e.t.c. you should always select does which are successful breeders, as like all characteristics, it is genetic. Obviously this cannot be determined at 6 weeks, but any does that lose litters or do not get pregnant when mated should be given no more than three chances to breed successfully, no matter what other characteristics they have. This sounds really harsh, but is a basic principal that has been followed in livestock breeding for thousands of years. After 35 years of selective breeding, we very rarely lose litters, we only lost 2 litters in the whole of 2017.

And remember, stick to the rules; be selective.

Chapter 2

A Coat of many Colours

As the Netherland Dwarf is a miniature of the many breeds of domestic breeds of rabbit that exist, it stands to reason that there are many colours to choose from. Indeed, the dwarf standard states that all colours can be accepted as long as they conform to the normal pattern of the accepted breeds. This even includes the agouti, a dwarf of "wild" rabbits. What is important is to choose your colour carefully and do not mix the colours indiscriminately. If you do you will lose the clarity of the colour dwarf breeders have been perfecting for over 70 years. Even though we are looking for a type animal, and colour is only 15 points in the standard, the colour is also important if wanting to push for the top honours at a show. It is important to do your research, Over the years more breeders have worked to improve type and colours on certain varieties so they pose less of a challenge when it comes to breeding youngsters that are showable. Whilst the rarer colours prove more of a challenge, it is really up to the individual which colours they prefer. Attending a National Netherland Dwarf Rabbit Club Stock Show is the best way to see more of the colours available and chat to the breeders, in an effort to make the correct choice for you.

Choosing the correct stock

There is a wealth of information on the internet and in many previous yearbooks about getting your foundation stock. They all pretty much revolve around the same theme; you should always go to a reputable breeder and purchase the best that you can afford. Whilst this is good sound advice, there are additional factors that need to be taken into consideration, firstly do a bit of research into the colours, there are over 20 colours commonly shown. Using the internet is a good place to start, but you should visit shows, especially dwarf stock shows, where you can see the colours on offer, and breeders of the colours that you like. Don't rush into anything, talk to the exhibitors, contact the secretary of your area dwarf club and the National Dwarf secretaries for advice. Your area secretaries will be able to put you in contact with breeders of specific colours in your area, much better than the National Secretaries who may well live hundreds of miles away. Be clear on your choice of colours and stick to it, you need to specialise on one or two compatible colours at first. Most experienced dwarf breeders will tell you just that, but we have all been through a stage of keeping too many colours.

The colours

The colour standard groups all dwarfs into one of 5 sections. Selfs are solid colours, such as Red Eyed Whites, Blacks, e.t.c. The shaded section, which are similar to the selfs in appearance, but they have darker colours on the head and back and get lighter towards the belly, example include siamese sable and siamese smoke. Agouti pattern has banded hair shafts consisting of three colours, such as agouti (wild rabbit colour) and chinchilla. Tan pattern has a range of different body colours, but they all have a white belly, white eye circles, white inner ears, such as black fox, marten sable and otter. The final category is any other colour, which consists of the colours that don't fit any other groups such as Himalayans, white with coloured ears, feet and nose, steels, orange, etc.

Again, the genetics of all the colours has been written about many times, there is an excellent article in the 2013 National Netherland Dwarf Rabbit Club Yearbook, a copy of which is available by contacting the secretaries. So without delving into the world of DNA and chromosomes here are a few tips on breeding the correct colours to be successful.

REWs are actually a coloured dwarf that carries a pair of alleles (specific genes) that prevent any colour from being expressed, so they have white fur and pink eyes. That means that two REWs mated together will always breed REWs. However breeding them to coloured dwarfs means that offspring will only have one copy of the gene that prevents colour, so the offspring will be coloured, what colour depends on the coloured parent and the hidden colour of the REW. So it is important if you are going to use REWs in your breeding of coloured rabbits, you know what colour it is genetically. We use siamese sable and siamese smoke REWs to breed into our sables and smokes, but not too often as that will increase the number of REWS born. BEWs, like REWs carry two alleles that mask the colour, when bred to other colours you will get a Vienna marked dwarf or mismarked. These dwarfs carrying one copy of the gene can be bred back to your BEWs to produce BEWs.

The genetics behind the other colours is more straightforward, with fewer hidden genes. As a general rule in the self section, any of the other self colours can be bred together. Similarly in the shaded section, sables, smokes and sealpoints are compatible, and torts to some extent,

although blacks are often used in tort breeding. Don't forget that unlike sables where the dark shade is showable, that is not the case in smokes. The dark smoke has a place in your breeding programme, but not for showing. Himalayans come in four colours, black, chocolate, blue and lilac. The Himalayan is actually a shaded rabbit, only showing the colour on the extremities. Therefore the black is actually dark sable, the chocolate, a medium sable, the blue, a dark smoke and the lilac, a medium smoke. Using the sables and smokes in the breeding programme can be useful to improve both colour and type.

In the agouti pattern, chinchillas and squirrels are compatible, agouties can be bred to them to improve type or banding in the coat, but don't use them too much as you will affect the colour. The main problem with the colour in agouties is the lack of a bright orange band. I personally believe that this is due to them being used in otter breeding. Opals are a dilute agouti, the black being replaced by blue in the hair shaft, and are often kept by agouti breeders.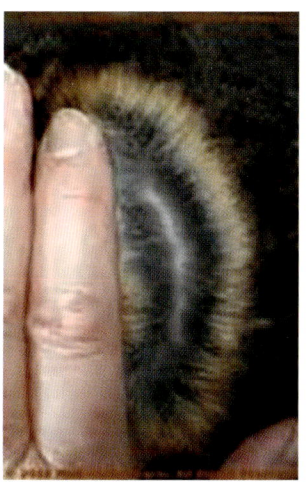

Like the shaded group, some of the tan pattern dwarfs can be bred together, marten sables and smokes, remember dark smokes are not allowed. I would not advise breeding otters or foxes to the martens, the shading in the martens will be lost as will the rich black colour of the otters and foxes. Many breeders breed marten and siamese sables or smokes together, the main reason is to reduce the white ticking on the martens, which can become too bright.

I have mentioned most of the common colours, there are lots more, and the breeders of those colours would be more than happy to go through them with you.

In conclusion, don't keep too many colours, be critical of your stock and talk to experienced breeders.

Chapter 3

Group 1 SELF

White

As pure a white as possible, creamy or yellow tinge a fault.
Eye colour ruby red OR rich dark blue.

Red eyed white: Genetic code ????cc??????

Breeding combinations: As the REW is an albino of another colour, REW bred to REW will breed REWs but is important to know what colour the REW is bred from if it is to be used to breed other colours, for example a shaded bred REW can be bred to shaded pattern dwarfs and so on.

Blue eyed white

Genetic code ??????????Vv

Breeding combinations: BEW to BEW will reduce the chance of breeding non showable colours. Many breeders introduce other colours into their BEW breeding programme to improve type and coat, this will produce Vienna marked rabbits. Vienna marked rabbits bred back to BEWs will produce a mixture of BEW and Vienna marked rabbits.

Black

Rich lustrous black, slate blue undercolour, brown tinge a fault.

Genetic code aaB?C?D?E?W?

Breeding combinations. Black to black, blue, tortoiseshell, agouti, black and blue otter.

Always select blacks that are black all the way down the hair shaft and with dark nails. Many blacks carry a fly back coat which flies back to its original position too fast when brushed in the opposite direction, so those with the correct roll back coat should be selected.

Blue

A clear, bright, medium shade of blue (not lavender) throughout, from tip of fur to skin.

Genetic code aaB?C?ddE?W?

Breeding combinations. Black, blue, agouti, opal, blue and black otter.

Always select blues that are dark blue all the way down the hair shaft and with dark nails. As blues are a dilute colour, they often suffer with light coloured nails, blacks with dark nails can be used to darken the nail colour

Brown

A rich dark chocolate, colour going well down the fur with a pearl-grey undercolour.

Genetic code aabbC?D?E?W?

Breeding combinations. Brown, lilac, lynx, brown and lilac otters

Always select browns that are a rich dark brown colour all the way down the hair shaft

Lilac

A pinky dove-grey throughout from tip of fur to skin. Bluish tinge a fault.

Genetic Code aabbC?ddE?W?

Breeding combinations. Brown, lilac, lynx, brown and lilac otters

Always select lilacs that are lilac all the way down the hair shaft and with dark nails. As lilacs are a dilute colour, they often suffer with light coloured nails, browns with dark nails can be used to darken the nail colour

Red

Top and Belly colour: top colour intense orange/red extended brilliantly over the whole body without visible change towards the belly colour. Belly colour and underside of tail slightly matt. Colour to be free from ticking. Eye colour brown. Nails to be dark horn colour. Whiskers must show an orange pigment. Undercolour: the intensively orange/red undercolour should stretch right down to the skin. The further the undercolour stretches the better.

Genetic code A?bbC?D?eeww + rufous modifiers

Breeding combinations. Red, red agouties and all colours of tan.

Always select reds where the colour extends all the way down the hair shaft, including the belly colour and with dark nails.

REWs are by far the most popular colour in this section, but they are undoubtedly the marmite of the dwarf colours, you either like the red eyes or you don't. When the dwarf was first introduced into the UK, and in the early years REWs were the colour, the classification at dwarf shows was REW and any other colour. In the 1980s it wasn't uncommon to have 40 in the REW buck class at the ASS. Sadly this is not the case in recent years, mainly due to the much wider variety of colours now available. Another factor is that pet shops don't want lots of REWs (the marmite effect) so passing on surplus youngsters that don't make the grade for showing is more difficult.

Standard requires the colour to be as pure white as possible from head to toe, literally, including the bottom of the feet. Therefore show preparation is important when keeping and showing REWs. To make life easier, clean rabbits should be used for breeding not those who like to scratch the bedding continuously, yellowing the feet. Often REW breeders have the dilemma of breeding that super typed dwarf, excelling all departments, but he doesn't keep himself clean. Not using that buck in the breeding pen is an easier decision if it is one of many that you have. If it is the best you have you may have to use it, but to does that are clean. Of course, cleaning out should be regular, many breeders take out the dirty corner of their REW show bucks several times per week, some do it every day. REW breeders often use a range of products to whiten the feet; not having kept and shown REWs, I am not the expert, so if that is your colour, chat to other REW breeders for their advice.

The advantage of the REW is that REWs breed REWs, but beware, some are not as white as others, some have a creamy tinge. As discussed in later chapters, they have their uses in coloured breeding programmes.

BEWs have challenged dwarf breeders for a great length of time, although a few dedicated breeders have improved their standard with commitment to the colour. Many imports from the continent have been used and the main challenge has been to selectively breed them to produce a dwarf that fits the UK standard for type. The continental dwarfs lack the depth of body, they are longer in body, ears tend to be carried backwards and they have a longer coat. Having said that, there have been excellent examples shown over the years. In order to breed BEWs other colours are used, resulting in Vienna marked dwarfs in the first generation, which are then bred back to the BEWs, so extra hutch space is required to house them. So if you fancy a challenge, they could be the colour for you.

Blacks are a surprisingly difficult colour, the challenge being to get a pure deep lustrous black, rather than one with a brown tinge. However, even the best coloured blacks will go dull and develop a brown tinge towards the end of the show season. All coloured dwarfs are prone to white hairs, but blacks show this more than any other colour. The final problem is the colour of the pads, the pads will be grey, but there is so much variation in the shade of this grey, the lighter grey looks almost white on a black rabbit.

Chocolates or browns have become far more common in recent years, mainly due to imports from Holland, and as with the BEWs, many of the chocolates exhibited still have continental features. There are a few breeders working to develop the colour to fit more closely to the UK standard. In my opinion there is still a way to go, but there are definitely signs of progress, with some very pleasing exhibits being shown.

Blues and lilacs, like the chocolates are bred and shown by a very small nucleus of exhibitors, so the best place to see them is at a stock show. As a dilute colour they do suffer from a lack of pigmentation in the nails, which must be selected against in the breeding programme. Also, they are prone to having longer softer coats that lack the required resistance to roll back into place. Having said that, they are both very attractive colours and deserve their place on the show table.

Reds are a new colour in the UK, bred by just a couple of exhibitors at present; I predict a big future for them.

Chapter 4

Group 2 Shaded

Sable (Siamese) Medium

To be a very rich sepia on ears, face, back and outside of legs and upper side of tail, the saddle colour shading off to a considerable paler colour on flanks and belly, the dark face colour to shade off from eyes to jowl to blend with the chest and flanks, all blending to be gradual, avoiding any blotches or streaks and consisting of a soft and varied diffusion of sepia shadings. The dark colour on back to extend from head to tail. The chest to be of the same colour as flanks and the whole fur to be absolutely free from white hairs. The undercolour to match the surface colour as closely as possible, following the varied shadings throughout.

Sable (Siamese) Light - As medium, but colour to be 'Rich Sepia'.

Sable (Siamese) Dark - As medium, but colour to be 'Very Rich Dark Sepia'.

NB The main difference in the three colours is the width of saddle in tone and intensity of Sepia colour.

Genetic code:
light and medium aaB?cchl?D?E?W?,
dark aaB?cchlcchlD?E?W? or aaB?cchlchD?E?W?

Breeding combinations. Siamese sable, siamese smoke and REW from shaded parents. Marten sable and marten smokes only if marten sables and marten smokes are wanted.

As sables are prone to uneven moulting, select breeding stock that moults quickly. Ensure that dark sables are not too dark or that they lack shadings.

Smoke Pearl (Siamese)

The saddle to extend from nape to tail to be smoke in colour, shading to pearl grey beige on flanks, chest and belly and to be totally free from white throughout. Head ears, feet and upper side of tail to match saddle as near as possible. All shading to be gradual avoiding blotches or streaks, general undercolour to match surface colour as closely as possible following the varied shadings throughout.

NB. Unlike siamese sables, the dark shade is not accepted for exhibition.

Genetic code aaB?cchl?ddE?W?

Breeding combinations. Siamese sable, siamese smoke and REW from shaded parents. Marten sable and marten smokes only if marten sables and marten smokes are wanted

Using medium siamese sables in the breeding of smokes will maintain the shading required.

Seal Point

A rich dark sepia brown on ears, nose, feet and tail. Shading to be a lighter colour on the body. Eye colour to be dark brown

Genetic code aaB?chlD?eeW?

Blue Point

Cream body with a blue mask, ears, feet, tail and shading on the lower rump and haunches, which blends into the body colour of cream on the saddle.

Genetic code aaB?chl?ddeeW?

Chocolate Point

Cream body with a chocolate mask, ears, feet, tail and shading on the lower rump and haunches, which blends into the body colour of Cream on the saddle.

Genetic code aabbchl?DdeeW?

Breeding combinations. Sealpoints, blue points and chocolate points

Pointed faults – Blotchy colour on body. Body colour too light or too dark so as to lose the decided contrast between the body colour and the marking colour. All colours are prone to a light tail which should be selected against in the breeding program.

Tortoiseshell (formerly) 'Madagascar' or 'Sooty Fawn'

Rich orange saddle, gradually shading to a blue black on the flanks, haunches and belly, 'Points' bluish-black. Top colour to go well down the fur with a bluish-white undercolour.

Genetic code aaB?C?D?eeW?

Chocolate Tortoiseshell

An even shade of orange top colour to carry well down and shading off to a lighter colour to the skin. Ears, belly and underside of tail – light chocolate brown. Cheeks and hindquarters (flanks) shaded or toned with light chocolate brown. Eyes brown.

Genetic code aabbC?D?eeW?

Breeding combinations. Black, brown and tortoiseshell.

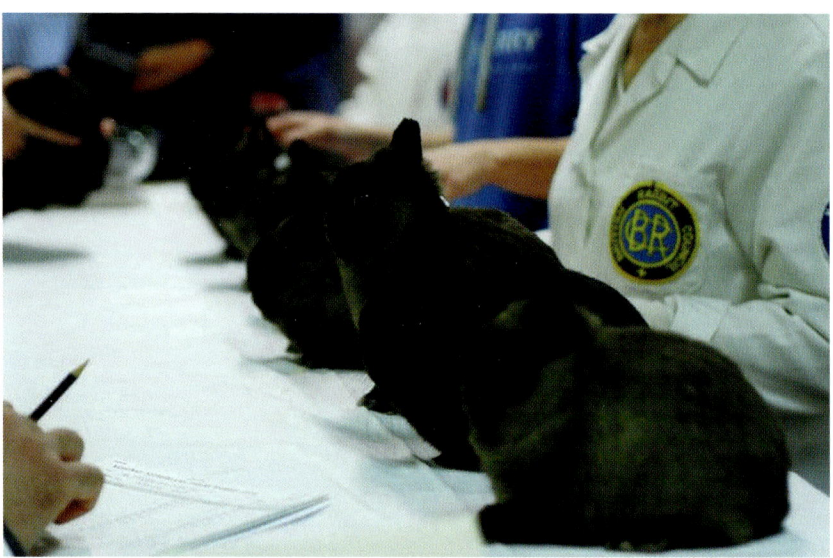

Siamese sables are the most popular colour in this group, and as many of you know, my favourite colour. There are three recognised shades, but the medium and light shades are genetically the same, only modifying genes determining the final colour so often merge together. As a shaded colour they have to show a gradual change in the colour from top to bottom, with the belly colour being the lightest. The main problem is that the dark shades are often so dark that it is difficult to see the shading. The medium is more common on the show bench, and generally more successful as more judges prefer them, penalising the dark ones due to a lack of shading. Genetically the medium and light carry a REW allele (gene) so it is common to breed REWs in your nests of sable. The dark sable doesn't carry a REW allele so they should be used in the breeding programme to reduce the number of REWs in litters. These sable-bred REWs can be used in the breeding programme but sparingly if you don't want to become a REW breeder. The major issue with the shaded group is the patchy coat that results if they don't moult properly, so again those that moult faster and completely should be selected for. Many exhibitors keep both siamese and marten sables and breed them together quite happily. The marten pattern is dominant so you will breed more marten sable than siamese sables. If you are interested in breeding siamese sables I would advise that you avoid using marten sables, we have kept purebred siamese sables since 1979 and never introduced a marten. A popular misconception is that the siamese will carry marten genes but this isn't possible as the siamese is recessive. There is a place for the siamese sable to help with marten sable breeding. If marten sables are bred continually the offspring will gradually inherit more and more white hairs making them too "bright". Using a siamese sable will reduce the volume of white producing the right balance between sable and white.

Siamese smokes again come in the three shades but only the light/medium shade is showable, this is because the colours of netherland dwarf follow the colour standard of the full size breed. There are some people who think that the dark shade should be showable, personally I don't agree. As with the sables, REWs will be bred from the medium shades. The dark smoke can be used sparingly in the breeding programme, but care should be taken not to use them too much so you don't breed too many un-showable ones. As dark smokes are not widely used for breeding, there will be a higher proportion of REWs in the nest. We breed our lightest siamese sables in our smoke breeding programme, as the smoke should be a dove grey, the sable helps to produce the correct colour of smoke. Many people use REWs to lighten their smokes, as previously mentioned, you have to know the colour that the REW is hiding. It would disastrous to introduce a black otter, it won't help your smokes. I would like to clear up one popular misconception at this point. Colour bred REWs do not introduce white hairs into coloured dwarfs. The REW is a coloured dwarf that has the colour "switched off" so if it is bred from rabbits that don't have a white hair problem, it will not carry the alleles for extra white hairs.

Sealpoints and tortoiseshells are the minority colours of the group, again only seen at stock shows with the odd exceptions. The major fault with both these colours is the presence of white hairs in the underside of the tail. This is also found in siamese sables but with careful selective breeding is relatively easy to eradicate. There are insufficient sealpoints and torts with dark tails to enable a quick fix. Also there is a wide variety of shades in both colours. Just like the siamese smoke, only the medium shade is showable, the darker shades are useful for breeding as they often have the required dark tails. As with the chocolates and lilacs, very few breeders have taken up the challenge. If this is the colour for you, you would be more than welcome to join the group.

Chapter 5

Group 3 Agouti Pattern

Agouti

A rich chestnut shade with black ticking over an intermediate orange band and a dark slate blue undercolour. Ears laced black. Eye circles, underside of tail and belly to be white with slate undercolour.

Genetic code A?B?C?D?E?W?

Breeding combinations Agouti, black, blue. Opal, black otter and blue otter.

A wide range of colours exist, select those that have a medium chestnut colour and a clearly defined banding pattern.

Opal

Top colour pale shade of blue with a fawn band between this and a slate blue undercolour. Ears laced blue. Eye circles underside of tail and belly to be white with slate undercolour.

Genetic code A?B?C?ddE?W?

Breeding combinations Agouti, blue. opal, and blue otter.

Select those with dark nails and free from a white undercolour, which should be slate blue.

Lynx

Top colour to be Fawn interspaced with Lilac. An intermediate Fawn band over a white undercolour. Eye circles, under of tail to be white with a pale lilac undercolour.

Genetic code A?bbC?ddE?W?

Breeding combinations Lilac, lynx and cinnamon.

The lynx is a lilac agouti so as a dilute they are prone to light nails so select those with dark nails.

Chinchilla

To resemble the normal chinchilla the undercolour to be dark slate blue at base, intermediate portion pearl (slate to be definitely wider than pearl) with black narrow line edging, pearling to be clearly defined, top grey, brightly ticked with black hairs, either even or wavy ticking admissible, neck fur lighter in colour than body but strictly confined to nape; flanks and chest ticked with uniform shade of pearl slightly lighter than body; eye circles light grey - pearl, well defined, ears laced with black.

Genetic code A?B?Cchd?D?E?W?

Breeding combinations   chinchilla, squirrel, agouti, opal, black fox and blue fox.

Squirrel

A sparkling blend of blue and white with blue ticking over an intermediate pearly white band with a light slate undercolour. Ears laced blue. Eye circles underside of tail and belly to be white with light slate undercolour.

Genetic code A?B?Cchd?ddE?W?

Breeding combinations chinchilla, squirrel, agouti, opal, black fox and blue fox.

Cinnamon

A rich cinnamon colour with a brown ticking over an intermediate orange band and lilac undercolour. Eye circles underside of tail and belly to be white with a lilac undercolour.

Genetic code A?bbC?D?E?W?

Breeding combinations   brown, agouti, chocolate otter, chocolate fox

Red Agouti

A rich red chestnut colour, much deeper in colour than the normal agouti body colour as agouti. Body colour as Agouti but with deep orange/red banding. Ears laced black. Toe nails to be very dark horn colour (near black). Belly colour cream to sand red, blue undercolour to belly to be treated as a fault, except in the groin.

Genetic code A?B?C?D?E?ww+ rufous modifiers

Breeding combinations   red agouti, red, all colours of tan.

Agouties are the leaders in this group in terms of popularity, although the chins are catching up. Agouties are generally of good type and do very well on the show table. With all members of this group the major issue is the colour, many suffering from a very pale narrow orange band. As a judge I have judged many agouti classes which have the ideal dwarf in it, unfortunately it is divided between several exhibits. Those with good type lack colour and those with the colour lack the type. Agouti breeders find this so frustrating, but they like the challenge. It is also important the white undercolour of the belly doesn't spread up to the chest. Another common fault is barring of the front feet, this is lighter patches on the front feet. The agouti was one of the first coloured dwarfs to be shown and as a result was used to develop many of the other colours shown today. This is probably the main reason why good coloured agouties are few and far between. I was going to say that agouti is an easy colour for the newcomer but after writing this I'm not so sure. If you are interested in agouties try to purchase from someone who has pure bred agouties where possible.

The opal suffers from the same colour versus type battle of the agouti, but as dilute colour the colour is often too pale and lacks the definition between the three colours on the hair shaft. Young opals are often born with the white undercolour throughout the coat, and they lose this when they moult their baby coat, just retaining it on the belly. Unfortunately some exhibits retain the white undercolour on their back and flanks. This is frustrating for the judge, as it doesn't fit the colour standard so should be penalised accordingly, but even more frustrating for the breeder/exhibitor.

The lynx is the lilac agouti, which has a white undercolour, orange intermediate band and the top of the fur is described orange shot silver, so the orange band should be topped with silver. As a minority colour not many judges get the chance to handle the lynx, this probably the reason why some are penalised for the white undercolour when in fact the blue undercolour should be penailsed. The dedication of just a couple of breeders has resulted in some excellent exhibits being shown under me, a real pleasure to judge them.

Chinchilla, see agouti… the challenge is to get the correct colour and type on the same rabbit. A dark slate blue, a pearl intermediate band and a black tip to the fur. The fur on a dwarf is approximately 1 ¼ inches so getting the three bands with the correct definition will always be a problem. In recent years continental imports have been used to improve the colour; as they are longer coated they often have the better colour. As already discussed previously it is important to get the type to match the UK standard. There is much debate about using agouties to improve the chins. My thoughts are the same for any outcross, if you need to improve a feature, either type or colour then bring in an outcross. If your chins lack colour or definition and you have access to an agouti with excellent colour and or definition, I would certainly use it, selecting the best coloured agouti offspring and breeding them back to the chins will restore the chin colour. I have chatted with my good friends Donelle Bomben and Tim Reese in America many times about this, and Tim always ends with the same phrase "There is no rush to perfect the dwarf."

The squirrel is a dilute chin and therefore lacks the definition of its dominant counterpart. Lots of breeders breed the two, using the chins to improve the squirrels. A light slate undercolour, pearly white intermediate and the top is described as a sparkling blend of blue and white. In my experience of handling and judging squirrels there are many excellent examples of really good type but they lack the "sparkle." Very recently a few continental imports with better colour are being used, watch this space.

The chocolate agouti or cinnamon is a very attractive colour and as it is not a dilute colour like the opal or lynx it is easier to get good definition. As with other members of this group it is a lack of breeders of the uncommon colours that is holding their development back, but there some really good examples of the breed being shown. They do suffer from the same colour faults as the more common agouti such as barred feet.

Chapter 6

Group 4 Tan Pattern

Tan

Body colour to be either black, blue, chocolate or lilac and to go down the fur as far as possible with undercolour of appropriate self-colour. Belly, chest, eye circles, inside of ears, underside of jowl and tail and triangle to be rich tan. Blue undercolour to belly to be treated as a fault except in the groin. Face and outside of ears to match body colour.

Genetic code;
black aT?B?C?D?E?ww and rufus modifiers,
blue aT?B?C?ddE?ww and rufus modifiers,
choc aT?bbC?D?E?ww and rufus modifiers
and lilac aT?bbC?ddE?ww and rufus modifiers

Breeding combinations, all colours of tan, red and red agouti

Fox

Body colour to be black, blue, chocolate or lilac and to go down the fur as far as possible with undercolour of appropriate self-colour. Chest, flanks and feet to be well ticked with white guard hairs. Eye circles, inside of ears, underside of jowl and tail, belly and triangle to be white.

Genetic code aT?B?chd?D?E?VV

Breeding combinations, all colours of fox, chinchilla.

Sable Marten Medium

To be very rich sepia on back, ears, face and outside legs, and upper side of tail, the saddle colour shading off to a paler colour on flanks, the dark face colour to blend with chest and flanks, all blending to be gradual avoiding any blotches or streaks and consisting of a soft and varied diffusion of sepia shadings, the dark colour on back to extend from nape of neck to tail. The chest, flanks, rump and feet to be well ticked with longer white hairs, white hairs or any extension of white ticking over sides and rump to be considered an added beauty and not a fault, but ears and saddle to be free of white hairs, the light nape of neck to be confined to a triangle behind the ears and to be as small as possible. Eye circles, inside of ears, line of jaws, belly and underside of tail to be white. General undercolour to match surface colour as closely as possible following the varied shadings throughout.

Sable Marten Light - As **medium** but colour to be rich sepia.

Sable Marten Dark - As **medium** but colour to be very rich dark sepia.

Genetic code: light and medium aT?B?cchl?D?E?W? and dark aT?B?cchlcchlD?E?W? or aT?B?cchlchD?E?W?

Breeding combinations. Marten sable, siamese sable, marten smoke, siamese smoke, As sables are prone to uneven moulting, select breeding stock that moults quickly. Ensure that dark sables are not so dark that they lack shadings.

Smoke Pearl (Marten)

The saddle to extend from nape to tail, to be smoke colour, shading to pearl grey beige on flanks and chest. Head, ears feet and upper side of tail to match saddle as near as possible. Chest, flanks, rump and feet to be well ticked with longer white hairs, the light nape of the neck to be confined to the triangle behind the ears and to be as small as possible. The eye circles, inside the ears, line of jaw, inside nostrils, inside of legs and feet, belly and underside of tail and triangle to be white. The colour under white belly fur should be fawn.

Genetic code aT?B?cchl?ddE?W?

Breeding combinations. Marten sable, siamese sable, marten smoke, siamese smoke,

Otter

Colour black, blue, chocolate or lilac, uniform colour to cover back and sides.
The underbody or belly to be creamy white also under the chin and tail. A
tan border to divide the white and colour and encircle nostril and under chin.
A mixture of body colour and tan covers feet. Tan ticking to the chest, flanks
and rump, extended ticking to be an added beauty not a fault. Tan eye circle
and nape of neck. The ears to be as body colour bordered on outside with tan
which covers inside of ears. Fault: a distinct lack of tan from proper parts.

Genetic code
Black; aT?B?C?D?E?W?,
Blue aT?B?C?ddE?W?,
Chocolate aT?bbC?D?E?W?,
Lilac aT?bbC?ddE?W?

Breeding combinations. Any colour of otter, black, blue, brown, lilac, agouti
and opal.

Marten sables are still a popular colour around the shows, in my opinion they are a good colour for a beginner as like their siamese cousin, they come in all three shades and don't have the problem of white hairs that the self and shaded group suffer from. As with the siamese, the medium is the most common shade, but the darks do look so impressive with the contrast between the dark sepia colour and the white belly, eye circles and inner ears. The white ticking should extend up the flanks, the more the better, this shouldn't be confused with standard white hairs. The white triangle behind the neck should be small, not extending too far down the back. As discussed in the shaded section, care should be taken not to breed marten to marten for too many generations as too many white hairs will spoil the appearance. The use of a siamese sable will help to rectify the problem. Although not common, I have seen marten sables with a putty nose, a white spot on the nostrils, which is a disqualification.

Marten smokes are less popular, the same applies as siamese, only the medium light shades can be shown. As a dilute, it is not uncommon for smokes to have very light nails. They should be horn coloured, not white, and it is very subjective as to whether a nail is white or light horn. Even though the marten sable and smoke are in the tan pattern group, they should still be shaded just like the siamese sable and smoke, dwarfs without the shading should be penalised accordingly.

Probably the most popular colour of dwarfs at the moment is the black otter. A rich black top, with a creamy white under belly and tan band separating the two and extending to circle the nostrils and under the chin, the eye circles and the triangle behind the neck. As the tan pattern gene is so dominant, this would account for the rapid rise in the number of otters that have appeared. Some exhibitors have bred their otters to marten sables, which does not benefit either colour. In essence it is breeding a shaded dwarf to a self dwarf. The litter will no doubt contain black otters or are they really dark marten sables? The only way to determine which of the two it is, is through several generations of test breeding. Much better to keep the two sections separate, in my opinion. Selfs can be used in the same way as siamese sables and smokes are used to complement the martens. All four colours of otter are showable, black, blue, chocolate and lilac. The same issues arise in otters as discussed in the self section.

Along with the otters there are all four colours of foxes. Not as popular as the otters, but with dedication of more breeders they could be. The blue and the lilac dilutes suffer from the same issues such as light toe nails. Many breeders breed black foxes with chins to improve the brightness of the foxes. As discussed in the agouti pattern section, the main issue with the chins is the poor definition, so using foxes will not help the chins.

The tan dwarf is certainly a rare colour; hopefully this beautiful colour will develop into the type to compete with the more dominant colours. It is really difficult to improve or even maintain the tan colour whilst trying to fix the desired type.

Chapter 7

Group 5 Other Varieties

Orange

Bright orange saddle shading down the flanks. Colour to go well down the fur with a white undercolour. Chest to match flanks. Eye circles, inside of ears, underside of jowl and tail, and belly to be white.

Genetic code
A?B?C?D?eeW?

Breeding combinations. Orange and fawn

Fawn

Warm fawn saddle shading down the flanks. Colour to go well down the fur with a white undercolour. Chest to match flanks. Eye circles, inside of ears, underside of jowl and tail and belly to be white.

Genetic code A?B?C?ddeeW?

Breeding combinations. Orange and fawn

Steel

To be bright steel throughout. Head, feet ears and belly to match body colours. Colour to be as free as possible from a brown tinge. Undercolour, dark slate, carried well down to the skin, with no trace of a grey or yellow band. Under colour of tail can be lighter. Faults: band in undercolour. Feet and ears not matching body colour. Barred feet.

Genetic code aaB?C?D?Es?W?

Breeding combinations. Steel, black and agouti.

Himalayan

Distribution of colouring as for the normal Himalayan rabbit. Ears black, nose black, even and well up the eyes. Front feet black and markings well up. Hind feet black to correspond with markings well up the hocks. Tail Black. The Himalayan Netherland Dwarf is recognised in all four colours, namely Black, Chocolate, Blue and Lilac.

Genetic code:
Black aaB?ch?D?E?W?,
Blue aaB?ch?ddE?W?,
Chocolate aabbch?D?E?W?,
and Lilac aabbch?ddE?W?,

Breeding combinations.
All colours of Himalayan, Siamese Sable, Siamese Smoke

Harlequin

Head to be equally divided, one side black one side golden orange. Ears one ear to be black and the other golden orange. The Black ear on the golden orange side of the face, and vice versa. Legs one front leg golden orange, the other black. One hind leg black the other golden orange, the reverse side to the front. Body to be banded in black and orange and clearly defined as possible. It shall not be considered a fault if the bands are broken at the vental and dorsal lines.Belly colour may be lightish. Colour, part dense black, part golden orange the brighter the better. The Harlequin Netherland Dwarf is recognized in all four colours namely Black, Brown, Blue and Lilac.

Genetic code:
Black and gold A?B?C?D?ej?WW,
Blue and fawn A?B?C?ddej?WW,
Chocolate and gold A?bbC?D?ej?WW and
Lilac and fawn A?bbC?ddej?WW,

Breeding combinations. Harlequins

Magpie

As Harlequin but the second colour is white rather than orange. The Magpie Netherland Dwarf is recognized in all four colours namely Black, Brown Blue and Lilac.

Genetic code
Black and white A?B?cchd?D?ej?WW,
Blue and white A?B?cchd?ddej?WW,

chocolate and white A?bbcchd?D?ej?WW and
Lilac and white A?bbcchd?ddej?WW,

Breeding combinations. Magpies.

The orange is such a difficult colour to get right, a rich orange colour shading down the flanks, the orange colour carried well down the hair shaft with a white undercolour. The common faults are a lighter face and ears and black ticking due to the agouti background. As with many of the rarer colours, the gene pool is so small, there is limited scope to outcross.

The fawn is a dilute orange and same issues apply, too few breeders and a limited gene pool. The same pattern as the orange but a warm fawn colour.

The steel should be a bright colour throughout with no brown tinge, and a dark slate undercolour carried well down to the skin. The under colour of the tail can be lighter, but not white, which is a major problem in steels. It is a slow process to eradicate as there are not enough with the correct coloured tails. The steels were much more popular in the 70s and 80s than they are today.

Himalayans are the most popular colour in this section, 4 colours. The beauty is in the contrast between the body colour and the colour of the points, the points should be as dark as possible. The points darken in colder temperatures, so they look much more attractive in the winter months. As the black himalayan is a dark siamese sable with the himalayan allele replacing the sable gene, the chocolate is a modified medium siamese sable, the blue is a dark siamese smoke and the lilac is a medium siamese smoke, those are the colours that should be used as an outcross not a black. The majority of the himalayans that I have judged over the years lack the boldness to compete at the top end of the table. I would be using the shaded dwarfs as an outcross to rectify the problem. The colour has improved a lot over the years and if more substance could be incorporated into the himalayans they would do really well.

Harlequins and magpies; the "ej" allele makes the orange and the colour split onto different hairs creating the bands of colour. Whilst it is possible to mate harlequin to a better marked harlequin to improve the markings, you can also use an agouti as the agouti has orange colouring and genetically they are very close. Some breeders feel it is better to use an orange as it carries the non extension gene which makes the colour sharper enhancing the orange. The magpie has the dark chin gene which replaces the orange colour with white, so why not use the chinchilla in your magpie breeding programme. These colours are such beautiful colours, it is such a shame that more people don't take up the challenge.

Breeding for success in the exhibition Netherland Dwarf

Chapter 8

The C Genes

To produce and maintain the colour of dwarfs that you want, it is much easier if you have a basic understanding of the genes that produce the desired colour. Genes are sections of chromosomes that code for certain characteristics. The colour of your dwarf is controlled by many genes and is therefore described as polygenic.

Inheritance of genes is a simple concept, inheriting one matching gene from each parent for the specific characteristic in the gametes (egg or sperm). A gene for a specific characteristic is called an allele. A Punnett square can be used to show the inheritance of the specific genes.

For example, using the letter A to represent an allele for a dominant characteristic and the letter a to represent a recessive characteristic, the alleles are inherited as follows:

Parent 1; genotype (the genes) AA crossed with parent 2; genotype aa, all the offspring will be Aa. So as A is dominant they will all show the dominant characteristic.

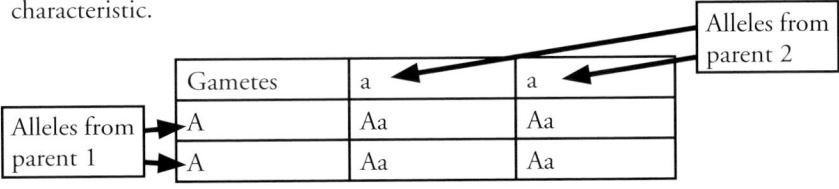

Gametes	a	a
A	Aa	Aa
A	Aa	Aa

The gametes are the eggs and sperm. The eggs or sperm carry one of the two alleles for the characteristic, so parent with a genotype AA will produce either an egg or sperm which all carry a single A allele.

Have a go at completing the Punnett squares to show the results of crosses between a parents of genotype (i) Aa and Aa and (ii) Aa and aa.

Gametes		

Gametes		

Now you are a genetics expert let's look at the C gene

C stands for colour saturation and is one of the more complex sets of genes, with 5 genes (alleles) in this set. They work to determine how saturated the colour is in the dwarf.

In order of dominance, the most dominant genes are "C," which is the full colour gene, "cchd," which is the chinchilla gene, "cchl," which is the sable gene, "ch," which is the Himalayan gene, and "c," which is the REW or albino gene, the least dominant.

The C allele is the gene that allows full colour, it is the most dominant, overriding the effect of any other allele it is combined with. So a dwarf with two C alleles (one from each parent) will have full colour, CC. A dwarf that has just one C allele and one of the other 4 possible C genes (see later in the chapter) will also have full colour , C?. Remember the Punnett square. The colour it has will depend on the genes it has for colour, e.g.Agouti, Black e.t.c. (another chapter!)

Opposite to the C allele is the c allele, stopping any colour being shown. This is recessive to all the other alleles in this set you need two c alleles to be an albino, cc. A REW or red eyed white, not a BEW or blue eyed white. There is another gene (v-vienna) that produces a blue eyed white (another chapter!). That means that all the REW dwarfs being bred and shown are genetically a coloured rabbit, but the presence of cc prevents the colour being expressed. So if you are using a REW in your coloured breeding programme you should know what colour it is!!!

Just when you thought it couldn't get more complicated, it does, there are also genes with co-dominance and incomplete dominance, and one gene that is affected by temperature. The three other genes (alleles) in this set: cchd, cchl, ch .

The cchd and cchl genes have co-dominance. Co dominance, as the name suggests is where the two alleles are equal to each other, when combined with another allele it causes a different appearance to either of the two pure breeding individuals.

The cchd is known as the dark chinchilla allele, which will allow the production of some but not all of the colour pigment in your dwarf. For example in an agouti, white bands will appear between the dark colour bands, producing a chinchilla, as the yellow pigment that is reduced to white. This gene can also affect eye colour and can produce rabbits with blue eyes. The full colour allele is dominant to this allele, so a dwarf with the combination CC or C cchd will be agouti, whereas cchd cchd will be chinchilla. The best coloured chins are produced when the dwarf is cchd cchd, pure breeding chinchilla, cchd ch, chinchilla carrying himalayan, or cchd c, chinchilla carrying REW, rather than a chinchilla carrying a sable allele cchd cchl. The sable gene shows incomplete dominance (see later) and tends to muddy the colour,

The cchl is the sable allele, or light chinchilla demonstrates incomplete dominance. Genes that show a normal dominant recessive relationship, if you pair them with the same gene or one of lower dominance, that gene is expressed, so the dominant colour is shown. With the sable gene, a pair of them together has a different result than the sable paired with a colour gene of lower dominance (e.g., "ch" or "c"). A dwarf carrying two sable alleles, cchl cchl produces a dark sable, like Bournville chocolate. This allele removes yellow from the hair shaft just like the dark chinchilla allele cchd, and some darker pigmentation, leaving the rabbit with a shaded look, although on the really dark sables it is sometimes difficult to see. Unlike the dark chinchilla allele, cchd, this gene always leaves the eye colour dark. Breeding two dark sables together will produce dark sables as the babies will inherit two cchl alleles, one from each parent..

A dwarf with one copy of the cchl allele will be a medium/light sable. If you breed two medium sables, which only have one cchl allele each, the babies could inherit a cchl gene from each parent and be dark, a cchl gene from one of the two parents and be medium/light, or inherit no cchl genes, inheriting two cc genes and be REW, hence the reason why siamese sable breeders produce lots of colour bred REW. They are just albino siamese sables. Using dark siamese sables as part of the breeding programme reduces the chances of breeding those REWs

The ch gene is the himalayan gene. This particular allele is activated by colder temperatures, preventing the production of the orange pigment seen in agouties (carotene) and causing heat sensitive melanin (dark pigment) production in the extremities, explaining why himalayans are better colour in winter.

A dwarf with two copies of the ch allele will be himalayan, ch ch or just one copy, ch c (carrying the more recessive REW allele).

In wild rabbits colour variations are as a result of random mutations, changes in the DNA, which if they give the rabbit an advantage in its environment, will allow more of the variants to survive, passing on the alleles for the mutation to future generations. The cold snow covered mountains of the Himalayas illustrates this principle. A white rabbit is better camouflaged than the agouti colour and dark extremities absorb more heat from the limited sunlight, preventing frostbite. More on the wonders of Natural Selection later in the book.

Chapter 9

The A Gene

The "A" gene comes in three forms: "A," which produces agouti dwarfs; "a^t," which produces tan pattern dwarfs; and "a," which is responsible for "self" dwarfs.

As there are three possible genes or alleles, these are called multiple alleles and your dwarf will carry any two of the three possible alleles.

As you know from the Netherland Dwarf standard, the Agouti pattern is made of a variety of different colours which all have this unique pattern; dark hairs, called "ticking," interspersed among their lighter middle coat. The base of the hair shaft is dark, causing banding to appear when you blow into the fur. Agouti patterned dwarfs have light cream to white markings on their belly, chin, inside of the legs, and bottom of the tail, dark lacing around the ear tips, and white circles around the eyes and nostrils, and white insides of the ears. The agouti pattern is the most dominant genetically. Members of the agouti patterned group include agouti, opal, lynx, orange, chinchilla, and steel. Orange and fawn dwarfs have what is called a non extension gene (ee) the non-extension ('ee') appears to erase the 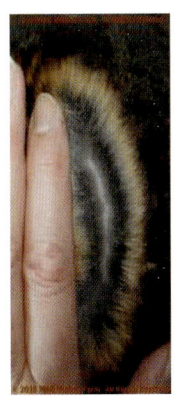 agouti banding so the dwarfs look like selfs ('**aa**'). Closer inspection shows that they do have the agouti pattern alleles, they have white bellies to the skin and do not have dark undercolour, this needs an article in itself. As the agouti pattern is the dominant allele (gene) an agouti pattern dwarf may carry two agouti pattern alleles (AA) or one agouti pattern allele and one of the more recessive alleles (Aa^t or Aa).

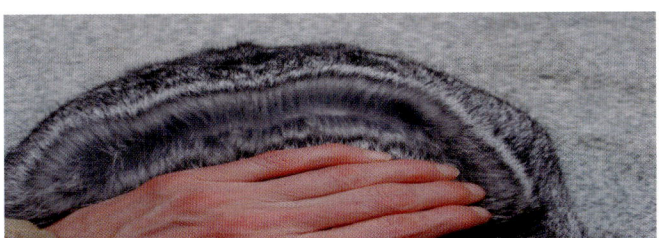

Below the agouti pattern is the Tan Pattern, (aᵗ). Tan patterned rabbits have a self or shaded colour on the top — like black, blue, chocolate, lilac, sable or smoke— and have lighter markings underneath, like agouti patterned dwarfs. Examples include otter, fox, marten sable and marten smoke and tan. A tan pattern cannot hide agouti as the agouti pattern is dominant, but it can hide the self gene. The genotype (genes contained) could be aᵗ aᵗ or aᵗ a.

The third allele in the A series is the self gene, (a). Self coloured dwarfs have the genotype of "aa," they cannot have the more dominant agouti or tan pattern allele. Black, blue, chocolate, and lilac. When we're talking genetics, the definition of self is slightly different. In addition to black, chocolate, blue, and lilac make up the self coloured section along with REWs and BEWs. The self coloured genotype aa can be modified to produce shaded dwarfs by the cchl gene.

There are different combinations of these A/aᵗ/a genes, remember you can have any two from the three choices, e.g. AA, A aᵗ, Aa, are all agouti pattern, aᵗ a, aᵗ aᵗ are both Tan pattern and aa is the self

Suppose you breed a pure bred agouti dwarf which carries two agouti alleles with an otter who carries the self gene. The Agouti is "A A", the otter is "aᵗ a,"

gametes	aᵗ	a
A	A aᵗ	Aa
A	A aᵗ	Aa

All the offspring will be agouti. If the agouti was carrying the tan pattern allele (A a^t) then the possible offspring would be different; There would be a 50% chance of getting agouties and 50% tan pattern.

gametes	a^t	a
A	A a^t	Aa
a^t	a^t a^t	a^t a

If you breed two otters that are carrying the self gene, out of every four babies, you could expect three to be otters and one to be a self. Two of those otters would carry the self gene while one of them would be a pure-breeding (homozygous) otter. Use a Punnett square like the ones above to show the cross.

Remember, self dwarfs produced from two such otter parents do not carry the "at" allele or the A (Agouti) allele. If a dwarf has the agouti allele, it will be expressed, i.e. the rabbit will be agouti pattern because it is dominant. If a rabbit carries the otter allele (a^t), the recessive self allele will be hidden.

There are other combinations of "A/at/a" genes. Test your new genetics knowledge by predicting the outcomes of a few crosses.

In this chapter I have referred to agouti pattern, tan pattern and selfs, rather than agouti, otter and black, because the genes covered determine which of the three groups the dwarf fits into. Individual colours in each group are determined by other genes, for example the B series. When combined with the "A/at/a" genes, B produces agouti, black otter or self black, b produces chinchilla, blue otter or self blue. The D series of genes are the dilution genes, so D produces no dilution, so the colours stay as listed above, but the d allele dilutes Agouti to cinnamon, chinchilla to squirrel, black otter to chocolate otter, blue otter to lilac otter, black to brown and blue to lilac. Referring back to the article in the previous chapter, which covers the C series of genes, all the above colours will be carrying the C allele for full colour, variations on this result in the various popular colours such as REW, sables, smokes and himalayans.

Chocolate Otter

Agouti Pattern (AA or A a† or Aa)	Tan pattern (a† a† or a† a)	Self (aa)
Agouti	Black Otter	Black
Opal	Blue Otter	Blue
Chinchilla	Black Fox	Self Chinchilla
Lynx	Lilac Otter	Lilac
Orange **	Orange or Tort Otter*	Black Tortoiseshell
Fawn **	Fawn Otter*	Blue Tortoiseshell

Italics; Not standardised colours of dwarfs in the UK.
**carry the non extension genes (ee)

Chapter 10

BED time!

Continuing from the articles in the previous chapters on the colour genes, here is the next instalment; the B, E and D genes; firstly the B gene.

Much more straightforward than the c genes, there are only two genes, B (black) which is dominant and b (brown / chocolate) which is recessive. As there are only two genes, there are three possible gene combinations: BB, Bb and bb. Remember one gene (allele) is inherited from each parent. As B is the dominant form of the gene (the dominant allele) BB & Bb will both produce a black dwarf, and bb will produce a brown.

Remembering the terms homozygous and heterozygous from the previous chapters, a black dwarf can be homozygous (BB) or heterozygous (Bb) whilst a brown can only be homozygous (bb).

The same principle applies to other colours, bb changes the black parts of the rabbit to brown.

Agouti based blacks:	Tan based blacks:	Self based blacks:
agouti AAABBCCDDEE steel AABBCCDDEsEs chin AABBcchdcchdDDEE orange AABBCCDDee	black otter atatBBCCDDEE black fox atatBBcchdcchdDDEE m sable atatBBcchlc/cchlcchlDDEE	s sable aaBBcchlc/cchlcchlDDEE self black aaBBCCDDEE black tort aaBBCCDDee seal point aaBBcchlcDDee black him aaBBchchDDEE
Agouti based browns:	Tan based browns:	Self based browns:
cinammon AAbbCCDDEE	chocolate otter atatbbCCDDEE chocolate fox atatbbcchdcchdDDEE	Self chocolate aabbCCDDEE chocolate tort aabbCCDDee choc him aabbchchDDEE

Next the dilution gene (D or d) which controls the colour intensity: a diluted black is a blue, and a diluted brown is a lilac. The dilution affects all aspects of colour, not just the hair colour. This includes the pigmentation in the skin and the eye colour.

Like the B genes, there are only two alleles in this set; D which gives full colour, and d, which produces the diluted colour. The D gene is dominant so if the dwarf has DD or Dd the rabbit will show full colour, and dd produces the diluted colour.

Agouti based full colour:	Tan based full colour:	Self based full colour:
agouti AABBCCDDEE steel AABBCCDDEsEs chin AABBcchdcchdDDEE orange AABBCCDDEe cinammon AAbbCCDDEE	black otter atatBBCCDDEE black fox atatBBcchdcchdDDEE marten sables atatBBcchlc/cchlcchlDDEE chocolate otter atatbbCCDDEE chocolate fox atatbbcchdcchdDDEE	siamese sables aaBBcchlc/cchlcchlDDEE black self aaBBCCDDEE Black tort aaBBCCDDee seal point aaBBcchlcDDee black himi aaBBchchDDEE self brown aabbCCDDEE chocolate tort aabbCCDDee choc himi aabbchchDDEE
Agouti based dilute colour:	Tan based dilute colour:	Self based dilute colour:
opal AABBCCddEE fawn AABBCCddee squirrel AABBcchdddEE	blue otter atatBBCCddEE blue fox atatBBcchdcchdddEE	Self blue aaBBCCddEE blue tort aaBBCCddee blue himi aaBBchchddEE

D = Full Strength
d = Diluted

So combining the chocolate and dilute alleles produces lilac based dwarfs.

– B- – D- – = Black (where the – represent A, C, and E)
– B- – dd – = Blue
– bb – D- – = Chocolate
– bb – dd – = Lilac

Agouti based lilacs:	Tan based lilacs:	Self based lilacs:
lynx AAbbCCddEE wheaten AAbbCCddee	lilac otter atatbbCCddEE lilac fox atatbbcchdcchdddEE	self lilac aabbCCddEE lilac tortoiseshell aabbCCddee lilac himi aabbchchddEE

The e series of genes

There are four alleles in this gene series:

- "ES" – Steel

- "E" – Full extension of colour

- "e" – Non extension of colour

- "ej" – Japanese brindling gene

The Steel (E^S) allele: The Es allele is the most dominant. Steel is only expressed (shown) if the rabbit also carries the A allele at the Agouti locus (position of the gene on the chromosome), i.e an Agouti. This is because the steel allele modifies the position of the Agouti hair bands on the hair shaft, leaving a silvery or golden tip to the hair. Dwarfs with the steel allele who are aa at Agouti locus, rather than AA or Aa, will be a self coloured dwarf as there are no Agouti bands present for Steel allele to change. Steel is also incompletely dominant so the correct 'steel' colour will only occur if the dwarf has a single **Es** and an E (EsE). If the dwarf is homozygous steel (E^{S}E^S) this will remove the Agouti hair band altogether producing a self dwarf. If you are breeding steels it is important to know that these self rabbits may be produced. They can be used in a self breeding programme but mustn't be sold as a black as they will ruin someone's black breeding programme.

The "E" – Full Extension of Colour or wild type

This is called the wild-type allele as it is the original Extension allele found in wild rabbits allowing the banding pattern on the Agouti hair shaft to be expressed. This colour has evolved over millions of years in wild rabbits to give them protection against predation as it is very effective camouflage. It is the most common of all the alleles in this gene series. It is recessive to E^S, it will only express if it is homozygous (EE) or if it is heterozygous with (Ee^J or Ee). Rabbits with this gene whether homozygous (E E) or heterozygous (E e or E ej) will have normal colour.

The "e" – Non Extension of Colour

The "e" allele determines how far out on the hair shaft the normal colour will extend. It reduces the extension of the colour along the hair shaft. For example a black (aa) that gets the "e" allele either homozygous (e e) or heterozygous with the recessive ej gene, the black colour will only extend part way down the hair shaft, so the shaft is mainly orange. Some shorter hairs remain all black and the longer hairs are more orange, resulting in a tort. If a dwarf has the genotype ee, and also carries wild-type agouti (A), it will be very pale agouti, due to lighter versions of red or yellow pigment.

The "ej" – The harlequin allele

The "ej" allele is the most recessive of the E genes. In the absence of other patterns, it causes black stripes or colour blotches in the coat. Harlequins will generally only be produced if homozygous (e^{j}e^j). The e^j allele is similar to the "e" allele but it affects the position of the colour on the rabbit not whether it is extended down the hair. Instead of the colour being non-extended on the hair shaft creating a tort, it non-extends in certain areas. This creates the harlequin or magpie pattern.

The En – The English marked allele.

Very confusing as this allele is not part of the E series, it is found in a different locus (position on a chromosome).

En, the broken pattern gene is dominant over en, the solid pattern gene, en. Therefore one broken pattern gene produces a broken, two broken pattern or En genes, you get a Charlie. A Charlie has a very small amount of colour in the white. Thus a solid rabbit is en-en, a broken is En-en and a Charlie is En-En.

Chapter 11

"It means nothing to me, Vienna"

The Vienna gene

Whilst REWs are full albinos, BEWs are incomplete albinos where the pigment melanin is restricted over the majority of the body. In REWs there is no pigment whatsoever in the eye whilst in the BEWs the pigment is not found in the stroma of the cornea (the middle layer) just the epithelium (the outer layer), full coloured eyes carry the pigment throughout all the layers of the cornea.

NNDRC

BEWs carry two copies of the Vienna gene (vv). It is generally thought of as a recessive allele but as it lies hidden in certain cases, there is still much debate. If you breed BEW to BEW you should get all BEW, but there have been cases of two blue eyed whites breeding REWs if the BEW is masking REW or himalayan. Also shaded colours and chocolates/lilacs that are hidden by the BEW alleles may produce BEWs with a ruby tint in their eyes, so it is best to avoid these colours into your BEWs, and of course if you are using REWs avoid those bred from shaded dwarfs or lilacs.

Thinking back to the dominance hierarchy in the C series of genes, cc produces a REW as it completely stops the melanin production when coupled with other genes. The Vienna gene does not stop melanin production entirely but allows a restricted amount of melanin across the whole of the body.

Breeding other colours into your BEWs will produce what are called vienna marked or Vienna carrier dwarfs. These are both genetically the same, Vv, the difference being the distribution of colour. The Vienna marked is a coloured dwarf with blue or partially blue eyes whilst the Vienna carrier will be white with blue eyes! If you breed together two dwarfs that are either of the above (Vv x Vv) then you will produce full coloured dwarfs carrying no Vienna allele (VV). The problem is that it is also possible to get a vienna marked dwarf with no white and not blue eyes. This is where records are vitally important as if these coloured offspring are sold on to breeder not wanting them for a BEW breeding programme, white patches and odd coloured eyes can crop up in future generations, so they must only be sold on for pets.

Chapter 12

Coat and condition

A fifth of the points (20%) are for these two features. As dwarf breeders and exhibitors we have had the luxury of good entries at shows, often having a separate dwarf section, and if we win the CC we are then more than happy to win best of breed. Personally, I feel that we have ignored the coat and condition for far too long, as we are "happy to win best dwarf and view anything as a bonus," which is why we are often beaten in the fancy challenges by other breeds. The opposing argument is that as dwarf breeders we are always at a disadvantage in the challenges because to get the best coat and condition we need to show a young adult dwarf. Traditionally, young adult dwarfs are not mature enough to compete in the challenges, so that puts us in a no win situation. This is changing, the gene pool of dwarfs in the UK has changed and we are getting dwarfs that compete for best of breed as early as 7 months, and are as such a perfect age to compete against other breed in the challenges.

Coat - Soft, short, dense, rollback. 10 points

As the standard says, we do not want long coated dwarfs, but as they often look bolder, they have gradually crept into some exhibitors breeding. Longer coats often lack density, there being a lack of under coat, so there is little resistance to your hand when the coat is brushed in the opposite direction. In addition, the longer coat doesn't roll back into position it does fly back into position. In recent years there have been a greater proportion of longer coated dwarfs being shown. These dwarfs are aesthetically very pleasing to the eye, the coat making the head look bolder and the shoulders wider. Whilst there are only 10 points for coat, a long coat is exactly the opposite of what the standard requires so if you are going to breed with them, it should be done with care, balancing the longer coat with a short coat. Genetically certain colours have harsher coats, the blacks and the black otters, but this does make them sparkle on the show table, and hence they are often found at the top end of the challenge. All dwarfs that are healthy should have a lustrous shiny coat. A moult free dull coat can be the first sign that something is wrong. More often than not the problem could be dietary related, so check that the water bottle is working and that the rabbit is drinking. Rabbits that are not drinking will not eat as rabbit pellets require unlimited water as they are a dried food.

Condition - Firm in flesh, good coat, free from any disease.10 points

It goes without saying that all of your exhibition dwarfs should be in prime condition, not just the ones that you show but all of your dwarfs. Condition is a characteristic that is influenced by many genes and is described as polygenic. Polygenic characteristics can be modified by environmental factors. Genetically your dwarfs will have an ideal weight, and at that weight will be in prime condition. If your dwarfs are underfed they will be underweight and therefore out of condition, whilst those that are overfed will be overweight and such obese dwarfs will often lack body condition. Of course some dwarfs will have a greater proportion of "large" genes and genetically be over the two and a half pounds, so restricting their food intake may get them on the show table, but out of condition. Pin bones are a contentious issue. Some dwarfs have a skeletal structure that the Ilium of the pelvic girdle is raised slightly higher than normal. So when you run your hand over the back of your dwarf you can feel the two bones protruding slightly. Some exhibitors and judges would argue that this means the dwarf is not firm in flesh, that it is out of condition, whilst others argue that the skeletal structure is not part of the condition. In the USA, there is much more emphasis on a smooth back end, and pin bones are frowned upon. The UK standard does not reference pin bones, so in its current form;it will always be a topic of debate. My own thoughts are that whilst I prefer a dwarf without pin bones, I would not penalise a dwarf for pin bones. There are three disqualifications that relate to condition; not in a condition of health to be judged, running eyes and overgrown or mutilated teeth.

Judges will assess the health of the rabbit whilst judging it, all they can look for are visible signs of disease. The skin is a very effective barrier to the entry of pathogens (disease causing organisms) and therefore provided there are no signs of the skin being broken or showing a mite infestation, the judge should examine the eyes, ears, nose, mouth and vent. These are areas that have a less effective barrier and therefore more likely to show signs of disease. Vent disease, although not common, is sometimes seen when judging. A rabbit with vent disease should never get to the show table as the exhibitor should examine the rabbits in the build up to the show and not show an infected rabbit. Many exhibitors will use a topical antibiotic application to treat the condition, (the treatment that is used for mastitis in cows). Whilst this will treat the symptoms it will not cure the condition, an injectable systemic antibiotic must be used which is only available on prescription from the vet. Running eyes should also be spotted before the show and therefore not reach the show bench. In many cases, the cause could be a small amount of fur trapped under the lower eyelid, which can easily be removed by lifting the lower lid away from the eyeball and removing the culprit. If this is does not cure the problem it could be a blocked tear duct, an infection or overgrown back teeth, all of which require a trip to the vet. It is almost impossible to check the back teeth but that is not the case for the front teeth. The top incisors should fit into a groove behind the front of the lower incisors. This ensures that both top and bottom incisors are worn to a sharp point and do not overgrow causing malocclusion. A hot topic of discussion in exhibition dwarfs is teeth that are not overgrown but the top incisors and the front bottoms ones meet, so the two are worn evenly producing flat or "level" teeth. In my opinion, this should not be a topic for debate; the teeth do not need to be overgrown to be incorrect. They should be correctly aligned. So please check your stock, and eliminate those level teeth from the breeding programme.

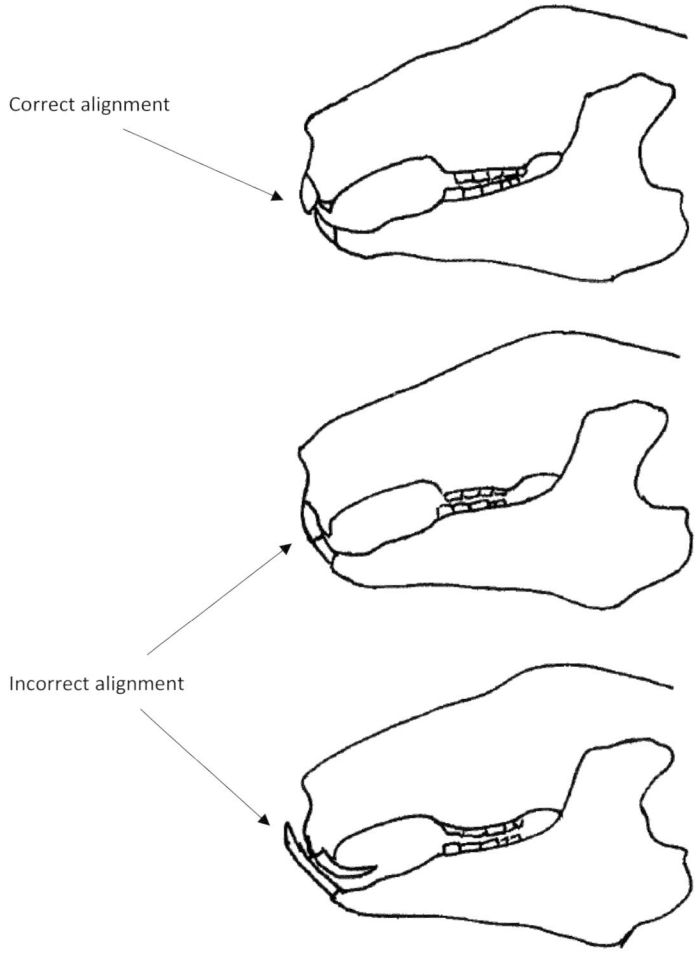

Correct alignment

Incorrect alignment

Good quality food and fresh water are so important in achieving and maintaining good coat and condition. All the successful studs will have their own regime that works for them so please chat with other exhibitors and then you can make informed choices. Firstly it is important that the rabbit gets unlimited fresh water as most people feed some form of dry food. The first sign that the rabbit isn't drinking is that it isn't eating. If you use drinking bottles, the spouts may become blocked with limescale, soaking the bottle tops in a kettle descaler will solve the problem. Bottles should be kept clean using a bottle brush; rabbits don't want to drink water containing green algae. The simple adage is don't let your rabbits drink what you wouldn't drink yourself. Some exhibitors put additives in the water, these are advertised in Fur and Feather, again ask around around before making your decision.

Over the years we have adapted our feeding regime. We now feed Masseys pellets (with ACS), rolled oats and readigrass (dried grass) in a 3:1:1 ratio. I am not a fan of rabbit mixes as dwarfs can be selective feeders, and often pick out certain parts of the mix. Each rabbit gets 2 ounces per day, measured using the cap from a furniture polish can which has been trimmed down to hold just 2 ounces. This is fed in the evening when I get home from work. Rabbits in the wild feed at dawn and dusk, so in addition they are fed hay every morning at 6am. Our rabbits also get a small amount of greens 3 times a week and a couple of barley rings once or twice a week. One thing that I have always done, following the advice of my mentor Alf Bottomley in the early days, is not feeding the pellet mixture one day per week, usually on the day before cleaning out. The rationale behind this is that in the wild rabbits may not always have food readily available so this mimics the natural behavior that they have to eat what is available. The rabbits will eat uneaten hay and any food that has been spread on the floor. The importance of a high fibre diet cannot be overstated, so ensuring that the rabbits eat more hay ticks the box. This also encourages the rabbits to search for their food, enrichment behaviour. There is an additional reason, as a Yorkshire man the cost of feeding six days a week is cheaper than 7 days! The key is consistency, changing your food regularly is not a recipe for success, so use what works for you and stick to it. You should feed a good quality feed that is easy for you to obtain. There is no point in choosing a brand that is a problem for you to obtain, as you may not be able to maintain a consistent feeding regime. Talking to exhibitors throughout my years of showing I am amazed how many have problems choosing the correct food, and as a result find it difficult to get their stock in prime show condition. I am sure that so many of these issues could be avoided if the exhibitor didn't keep changing their food.

Remember when buying stock it is always better to get some food from the breeder and then gradually change over onto your own feed. This will give the rabbit time to get used to the new ingredients, as the change to a new environment is stressful enough. It is important to monitor the weight of your dwarfs regularly and adjust the amount of food accordingly. The dwarf should feel firm, in good condition, not fat and certainly not thin so you can feel the backbone. Currently, the dwarf standard does not have an ideal weight, only a maximum weight of 2.5 pounds. As a judge, it is disturbing to be presented with dwarfs that are within the weight limit, but have obviously had their food restricted to make the weight. Dwarfs should be bred – not fed – to be the correct size and weight.

In addition to a good diet, exercise is important to get your dwarfs in prime condition and there are lots of opinions on the correct cage sizes for dwarfs. In order to allow our dwarfs to increase their exercise we put them into a wire pen on the lawn or the shed floor if the weather is poor. The added advantage is that they will mow your lawn for you. I do however think that we are in the minority when it come to this, most exhibitors don't put their dwarfs on the lawn. I can imagine all you REW and BEW breeders reading this with horror.

Your dwarfs will break into a moult during the summer months, and therefore cannot be shown. At this time it is important to keep handing them regularly to check their condition, we slightly increase the amount of food as the protein requirement increases at this time. Hair is essentially a protein called keratin, so replacing all that protein requires this higher protein intake, and carbohydrates and fats to provide the energy to make keratin. Brushing, combing and wet hands can be used to remove the old fur which helps to stimulate the growth of the replacement fur. Most people will not breed their dwarfs when they are in moult. I have heard exhibitors say that breeding with moulty rabbits will mean that the youngsters will always be in the moult. There is no genetic support for this. As exhibitors we should be breeding with dwarfs that moult quickly and thoroughly, as this is genetic. Avoid breeding with dwarfs that take an age to moult, as those alleles (specific genes) will be passed on.

Chapter 13

There are more points for " type"

Such a common phrase in the world of exhibition dwarfs, usually when a dwarf has been penalised for colour when being judged. Whilst colour is important, the type of a dwarf is the most important, there are 65 out of 100 for type and only 15 points for colour. Read the standard and familiarise yourself with the marks allocated to each feature. As dwarf breeders we are aiming to produce a dwarf with an overall shape that is far removed from the wild type rabbit. Fossil records suggest that Lagomorpha (the order that mammals belong to) evolved in Asia at least 40 million years ago, The European wild rabbit evolved around 4,000 years ago on the Iberian Peninsula. 'Hispania' (Spain) is translated from the name given to that area by Phoenician merchants, meaning 'land of the rabbits'. When the Romans arrived in Spain around 200BC, they began to farm the native rabbits for their meat and fur. The Romans called this practice 'cuniculture' and kept the rabbits in fenced enclosures. Inevitably, the rabbits tried to escape and that gave rise to their Latin name 'Oryctolagus cuniculus' means 'hare-like digger of underground tunnels'. Over thousands of years, evolution shaped the wild rabbit into a streamlined prey species that is perfectly designed to escape from predators. The modern dwarf has a bold round head with a bold eye and short ears of good substance, whereas the wild rabbit has a sloping narrow skull with much smaller eyes and long thin ears ideally suited for detecting predators and losing heat. Similarly, the body of a wild rabbit is long and narrow, with long legs, again evolved to escape predation.

EARS:
15 points -
Erect, of good substance,
well furred, slightly
rounded at tips. Desired
length 50mm (2 inches).

BODY:
30 points -
Short, compact, cobby,
full chested and wide
shouldered devoid of
raciness. Front legs
short and straight.

EYES:
5 points
- Round,
bold, bright
of good
colour.

HEAD:
15 points
- Round,
broad skull.

COAT:
10 points -
Soft, short,
dense,
rollback.

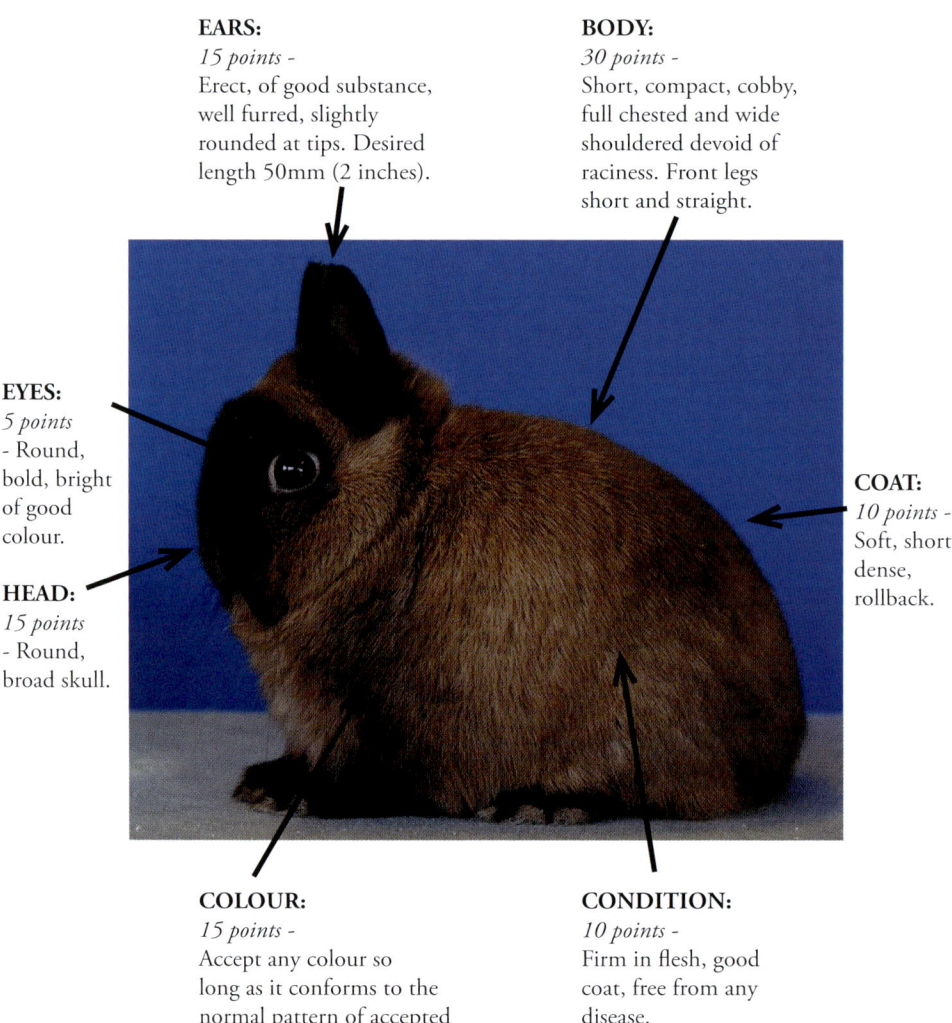

COLOUR:
15 points -
Accept any colour so
long as it conforms to the
normal pattern of accepted
colours of other breeds.

CONDITION:
10 points -
Firm in flesh, good
coat, free from any
disease.

Body - Short, compact, cobby, full chested and wide shouldered. Devoid of raciness. Front legs short and straight. 30 points

As the body carries the most points of any individual feature, it is important to get the shape correct, but it is the overall type that is important, often referred to as the balance of the rabbit. The body should be short and compact, with a depth to the chest. The head should be carried high on the shoulders giving the impression of no neck, not low on the front of the body. The National Netherland Dwarf Rabbit Club logo illustrates this very well. The overall type consists of two circles, and a straight line can be drawn straight down from the ears, to the front feet. From the front the dwarf should be wide chested with the front legs at the side of the chest, not unlike a bulldog.

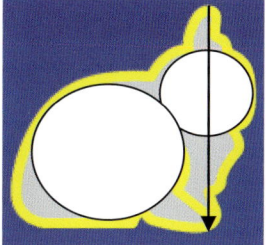

Many dwarfs exhibited are too long in body, some exhibitors and judges are very good at posing the dwarf to shorten the body. As a breeder you should select your breeding stock to shorten the body. Whilst the standard does not mention depth of chest, if the body is to be short, the spine has to be slightly more curved, and therefore the front of the dwarf sits higher. The head should also be set into the body and carried high up not low, as this would add length to the dwarf. There are dwarfs being used for breeding and showing that lack the depth of chest. The short front legs should be wide apart, which is only possible if the chest is wide, again this should be part of your selection process. When you put your hands over the shoulders of your dwarfs they should be wider than the hips, the hips should not stick out. Back legs are not mentioned in our standard, but if the hips are set properly then the back legs should be carried parallel uner the body. When turning the dwarf over, the back legs should not form a V shape, they should be short and parallel. This is a major fault in dwarfs and can lead to breeding problems which will be discussed later. As a newcomer, or experienced breeder you should always be looking to improve, be critical of your stock, visit other breeders and keep the discussion going.

It's all about circles!

Jan Lucas' diagrammatic interpretation of the dwarf

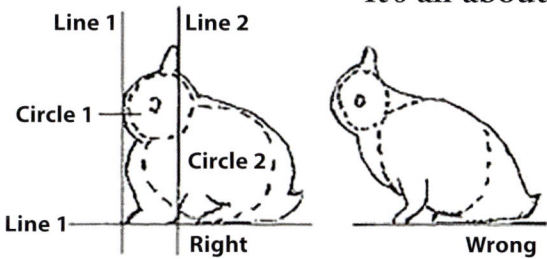

Circles applied to a successful dwarf of today

Ears - Erect, of good substance, well furred, slightly rounded at tips. Desired length 5cm (2in) 15 points

The ears should be of good substance, not thin and pointed. There is much debate about the substance of the ears, European and American dwarfs have ears which are really thick and are therefore described as having good substance. The term "spoon shaped" is often used. If you open the ear the shape should resemble your thumb or a teaspoon. From the side the ears should look open and not pinched together at the bottom. Ears that lack substance will not have the desired spoon shape and will be pinched. Ears should be held upright at 90 degrees. The standard does not say that but, ears that are held back make the head look elongated and not round like a tennis ball, improving the balance. Also ears that lack substance will often appear bowed from the front and although standard says they don't have to touch, they look better if they do, and lots of judges place a lot of emphasis on this. V shaped ears rarely win. There are no other features with regards to type which have a quantitative measurement to follow, so it is very easy to assess if the ears are the correct length. There is some debate however, is the measurement taken from the skull or from the top of the fur on the head? I have always taken the measurement from the skull. With experience, it is easy to spot ears that are longer than two inches. Personally, I confirm this by comparison with the length of my index finger from tip to the second knuckle, which is exactly two inches. Of course, unless your fingers are same length as mine, you will have to use a ruler or grow your nails!

Head - Round, broad skull. 15 points

The standard says it all, the skull should be round from all angles, a sphere. The boldness and position of the eye and the ear carraige are vital when it comes to assessing the shape of the head. As with all prey species the eyes are positioned on the side of the head. Side eye placement allows for greater peripheral or side vision. This enables the animal to see predators approaching from the side as well as from behind. This vision is very important for protecting an animal when it is grazing or feeding. An eye in the centre of the head make the head looks rounder, an optical illusion. Coupled with incorrect ear placement, the head can look very elongated.

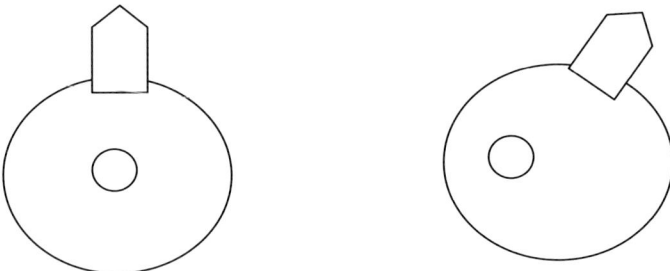

The head should be bold, it should be a broad skull when seen from the front. This is such a key feature as it is the first thing a judge sees when assessing the line up in front of them. Many judge's reports read "lacks width of skull" and even though the head is worth only 15 points, and a proportion of those must be allocated for the roundness, in most judges minds it is probably allocated more points than what it is worth.

Eyes - Round, bold, bright and of good colour. 5 points

The eye is only worth a few points, but as mentioned above it is such a key feature when combined with the head. A bold eye accentuates the shape of the head. This is even more evident in colours with eye circles such as martens and otters. A feature that is occurring more and more commonly in dwarfs is drop eye, when the white Sclera of the eye is visible around the coloured iris. Even though this isn't mentioned in the standard, the eye cannot be deemed to have good colour if it has a white ring around it.

Popular mis-interpretations of the standard:

There are more points for body so it is the most important feature!

Not necessarily; head, ears and eyes are worth more points, far too many exhibitors and judges are obsessed with the body. Whilst it is a very important feature, the overall balance is the key issue.

The ears should be together!

Not necessarily, the standard doesn't say that they should be together, it says of good substance, well furred and slightly rounded at the tips. However they do look far more aesthetically pleasing if they are together. The key is the correct ear shape and substance, which is part of the standard.

Eyes are only worth 5 points so they are not that important!

The eye gives shape to the head, the bolder the eye the rounder the head, dwarfs with bold eyes always have a round head. The moral of assessing your dwarfs and judging other people's is that you cannot take one feature in isolation, eyes must be "viewed" as part of a bigger picture. In tan pattern dwarfs the white eye circle enhances the eye shape, those that lack eye circles rarely win.

Dwarfs should be penalised with "drop eyes"

Why? It isn't mentioned in the standard, or in the disqualifications, but round bold and bright are, so these features should be looked for. The main argument against drop eyes is the white sclera if it is the eye is the wrong colour!

© NNDRC

Short, compact, cobby and wide shouldered is how most people read the standard.

This is how most people read the standard, the words full chested are missing! The front legs should be under the head and that is only possible with a full chest. A dwarf that lacks depth of body at the front cannot possibly be full chested. This is the major difference between the UK standard and the European dwarf standards. Many European dwarfs lack the depth so care must be taken if you are introducing them to your stud.

Chapter 14

Breeding to Win

For me, the best part about keeping exhibition dwarfs is breeding the next winning dwarf. Watching them appear from the nest at 3 weeks, identifying the "good ones" at 4 weeks, ringing them at 6 weeks and then looking forward to the first show pretty much sums up how easy it is!

The problem is that the dwarf rabbit doesn't breed true so it is so important to carefully select the breeding stock to fix the desirable characteristics.

Dwarf does will readily breed from about 6 months of age, the first signs will be the messy cage. The wet corner is now a thing of the past, the doe churning up all her bedding materials; she may even start nest building. On inspection her vulva will be swollen and dark purple due to an increased blood supply. In this condition she should readily mate, and should be introduced to the buck's cage. Rabbits can be territorial so putting the buck into the doe's cage may result in a fight. Rabbits have induced ovulation, which means the act of mating causes the release of eggs from the ovaries. To ensure the mating results in a successful pregnancy it is advisable to mate the does 3 or 4 times. After the first mating, remove the doe and wait 30 minutes before remating and repeat for a third mating. This should cause ovulation, the eggs released will pass along the oviduct or fallopian tube to the uterus. 12 hours after the initial mating we put the doe back to the buck to mate again.. The thinking behind this is that if the first matings didn't stimulate ovulation, this one will. If ovulation has taken place, there is now additional sperm to fertilise the eggs that are moving towards the uterus. Dwarfs are a difficult breed to breed successfully so any way to increase the success should be tried.

The doe does not need any additional food until the litter is born 31 days later. When she has littered I double her food so she can produce enough milk to feed the litter. I use nest boxes for the doe to litter in, which I put in the cage a week before she is due. The boxes I use are made of plywood, and measure 8 inches wide, 12 inches long and 8 inches high. My boxes have a floor, but some breeders use boxes without a floor, again personal preference. Our dwarfs are mated in groups of up to 4, so all the does kindle at the same time, this means that if a litter is born and the doe does not look after them they can be fostered. This is always a last resort, I always give the doe time to complete her nest, and check if she has any milk. If she has milk but hasn't plucked any fur I pluck her, this help to stimulate the production of more oxytocin, the hormone that stimulates the uterus to contract and milk production. If the doe has no milk or shows no interest, the litter is fostered. Remove the foster doe, put the youngsters in her nest and put the fur back over them. Put the doe back and feed her so she doesn't immediately investigate the nest.

IF the doe builds her nest and plucks after two weeks she is having a pseudo or false pregnancy. It may be that she has reabsorbed the youngsters or was never pregnant, In any case she should be remated and hopefully 31 days later she should kindle.

Some breeders mate their does on Wednesdays so they kindle on Saturday, when they are not at work when the litter are born, so can intervene if necessary, unless you are lucky enough to have retired! Personally I mate the does on any day, as they usually litter through the night and I am in the shed early in the morning, so it doesn't matter what day. Also, I am usually busier at weekends than week days; it must be because I am a teacher!

Some people don't let their does raise just one youngster, they foster it and remate the doe, rabbits will readily mate in the first two or three days after giving birth, just like their wild cousins. Other breeders remate the doe with one youngster and then she will litter when the lone youngster is 31 days old, sharing the cage with the younger litter, again natural behaviour. It is personal choice; find a system that works for you. It is important that does are kept for their mothering instincts, does that lose three litters are not retained for breeding.

We remate our does when the litter is 4-5 weeks old and wean at 6 weeks, giving the doe ample time to prepare for her next litter. As always, regular handling of all your stock not just the show bucks, is important. If a doe is out of condition due to raising her litter she is rested until she is back in condition.

 I check the litter the day that they are born and then leave them alone until they appear from the nest at about 3 weeks. The sign that the litter are doing well and are being cared for is a large fluffed up nest. One flat nest is often a sign of a lifeless litter. If the young appear to be dead I warm them in my hands and very occasionally this revives them and they can be fostered. Often the dead youngsters show signs of bruising around their head, and won't rally round if warmed. At the initial inspection I remove the peanuts as they won't survive. Once the litter appears I increase the food yet again, one portion (2 ounces) for each youngster and one for mum. It is important to check the eyes to ensure that they have opened properly, also the vent area. When they start eating solid food the faeces may stick to the rear end and should be removed. I assess the youngsters at 4 weeks and make a decision as to which will be staying. They are weaned at 6 weeks and any that are staying are rung. I always ring bucks on the right leg and does on the left leg. They are then put in pairs or threes and run on until 12-14 weeks when they are separated into individual cages. The stress of weaning makes the youngsters vulnerable to health problems, so vigilance is key. It is interesting to see how many that are keepers at 4 weeks actually stay. Our particular strain means that we are usually pretty accurate. Many breeders assess their stock later so have to run on more than we do. It is important to know your strain, so that you don't sell the next big winner as a pet! A common phrase that you will hear is that the youngster is going through its ugly stage, when it becomes gangly, usually between 7 and 14 weeks. Whilst this is true for many dwarfs, I believe that the real top class dwarf bucks that go on to have very successful show careers don't have an ugly stage.

An added complication is that some dwarfs just don't survive after they move onto solid food. This defect, where they just fade away, is not fully understood, but it is thought to be associated either with the dwarf gene or perhaps with a digestive condition. As it usually affects whole litters it is probable that there is a genetic component. These youngsters don't adjust to solid food, stopping eating and drinking: they hunch in a corner and grind their teeth. The condition begins around 4 weeks, but could also be as late as 6-12 weeks.

There is no right or wrong answer to how often should you breed your dwarfs. Most exhibitors that I know well do breed all year round, and the majority do breed specifically for the young stock shows in September. The National Netherland Dwarf young stock show is traditionally the 3rd or 4th weekend in September. As young dwarfs develop very quickly and change a lot from week to week, the aim is to show the under 5 month dwarf as close to 5 months as possible to maximise the chances of being at the top of the table. Mating the does to litter in the second half of April is ideal. Any does that miss or lose their litters can be remated to breed the dwarfs for the under 14 weeks classes at the YSS. If your choice is not to mate all year round but to rest the does over the winter months, it is advisable to mate the does early in the new year to have a litter before remating for the YSS litters. It isn't uncommon for a doe to be reluctant to mate after a rest, to miss or to lose the litter. The most common reason that does miss is that they are overweight. Lots of breeders reduce the food intake of their does prior to mating, substituting the normal food for hay for a few days. This mimics a rabbit's natural diet so is not an issue.

We don't use any form of heating in our shed; the rabbits all have fur coats so they don't need a heater, again personal preference. We do use heat lamps when does litter in the colder parts of the year. This maximises the chance of keeping the vulnerable new born kits alive until they grow their own fur coat. The original heat lamps PIR lamps with the lamp replaced with an old fashioned 40 watt bulb, reflecting the heat generated into the cage. More recently, they are made to order, and are available from the National Netherland Dwarf Rabbit Club (NNDRC). They hang on the cage front, the heat from a 40 watt coloured bulb gives out enough heat to keep youngsters alive that get pulled from the nest.

So now we have a foolproof method, what do we mate to what? Firstly you have to know the standard, have a picture in your head of what you want to achieve. For experienced breeders and exhibitors this is relatively straight forward as you will have handled lots of dwarfs over the years and the fact you have enjoyed this hobby for so long means that you must have been doing something right. However it is important not to get complacent, every breeder should always be looking to improve the quality of their stock, so be critical. For the newcomer, you should visit stock shows, steward for the judge and ask their opinion on their placings. Secondly, visit other breeders and get them to go through their stock with you, explaining their method of selecting what to breed to what.

There are fundamental principles that have stood the test of time:

- Rabbits with the same fault should not be mated together as you will double up the alleles for the faults thus fixing it into your stud.
- Never breed with dwarfs that carry a disqualification.
- Don't mix colours indiscriminately, breed together only compatible colours.

Another mistake that people make is to decide on the pairing, and for whatever reason the doe will not accept the buck, so they try the doe to a different buck just to get it mated. Be patient and try the next day. There are many techniques that have been used to get the doe to mate. These include: putting the doe in the buck's cage and vice versa for up to 24 hours, putting some of the buck's dirty bedding into the doe's cage, even leaving the buck and doe together for a week. In my experience, just being patient and introducing the doe to the buck's cage each day until she mates works. When looking for that continual improvement from generation to generation you must always assess the youngsters and keep those for breeding that are improvements on the parents. Some breeders score each rabbit giving a quantitative measurement of the characteristics. Whatever method you adopt, there must be a system and stick to it. It important that you retain your breeding does until their replacements breed successfully.

Every rabbit has two size genes, along with many other pairs of genes for fur colour, eye colour, etc. Each buck and doe will pass on one of their size genes to each of their young, so each youngster will have two size genes.

As the dwarf gene is dominant, a youngster with just one dwarf gene will produce a dwarf rabbit. However if the dwarf inherits two copies of the dwarf gene this is a fatal combination, without a normal gene as a recessive back-up, a rabbit who inherits two copies of the dwarf gene always dies.

The combinations of size genes that any rabbit could receive are :

- Dwarf and Dwarf, or...

- Dwarf and Normal, or...

- Normal and Normal

A double dose of the dwarf rabbit gene results in a "peanut."

This two-dwarf-gene combination is *always* fatal. It is thought that the double dwarfs have digestive and brain abnormalities.

Fig. 1. Peanut and normal dwarf.

If not stillborn, they usually last only 1-3 days past birth, although some may last up to a month. These peanuts are very small and can be easily identified at birth.

If you're breeding any of the dwarf breeds, you will always breed peanuts, which always die.

The rabbits that get one normal gene and one dwarf gene are known as true dwarfs, the ones that we want in the litters, hopefully matching the dwarf standard that we all breed to.

The dwarf rabbit that gets two normal genes is known as a false dwarf, not carrying a dwarf gene at all.

Fig. 2. The one on the right is the false dwarf, not much bigger that the true dwarf does, especially the one in the middle. All 3 does will be kept for breeding.

Because the Netherland Dwarf rabbit is a small breed to start with, the false dwarf, when born, is just a little bigger than normal, with slightly longer ears than normal, the body will be longer and gangly, and it will have longer feet. Netherland dwarf breeders call them "big ugly does."

Most BUB's - big ugly bucks - are sold as pets. You could keep the buck as part of your breeding programme, for use with a true dwarf doe, but it must be used selectively or you will introduce too many non-dwarf genes.

It is more common to keep the BUD - big ugly doe – to breed with, but only if her body type is promising (not counting the extra size). So you should keep the BUDs that are not ugly, just big, because remember, ideal dwarf rabbits have ONE dwarf gene and ONE normal gene. The BUD will contribute that normal gene to 100% of her offspring. Your stud buck will pass on 50% normal genes and 50% dwarf genes, so the probability is that you will breed 50% true dwarfs and 50% big uglies.

Figure 3. False dwarf (BUD) on the left, true dwarf doe on the right.
Both excellent mothers, false dwarf litter size averages 3.5,
true dwarf averages 2. Both does are 2 years old and have never lost a litter.
The false dwarf is the mother to the litter in Fig. 2.

If you breed together two true dwarfs the probability is that you'll end up with:

- 25 percent peanuts. These will all die, of course.

- 50 percent true dwarfs. These are your keepers.

- 25 percent false dwarfs. You might consider keeping a BUD (doe) as a brood doe. The bucks most likely you'll sell as pets.

If you breed a true dwarf buck to a 'big ugly doe' (false dwarf), you'll probably get:

- 50 percent true dwarfs (your keepers)

- 50 percent false dwarfs

So whether you use does that are true dwarfs or false dwarfs, if bred to a true dwarf buck, you'll end up with 50% true dwarfs.

Remember which genes that are inherited are totally random, there's no telling what combinations you might get of true dwarfs, false dwarfs and lethal peanuts in one litter, as the litter sizes are small. But over many litters, the probabilities work out

Another inherited condition found in dwarfs is Max factor, caused by recessive alleles and named after "Max," a famous Dwarf buck who first produced youngsters with this defect. Max Factor babies are born with deformed hind legs and their eyes are often open at birth, as though their eyelids were non-functional, along with other congenital defects that are not visible.

Most young frequently die within days, however some do survive, their eyes often fill with pus due to the damage caused by being unprotected. They are unable to move properly due to their deformities so should be put to sleep.

There could be a few advantages to using a BUD as a breeding doe:

- The larger doe may kindle more kits in a litter, increasing the odds for true dwarfs in a small measure.

- The larger doe may produce more milk.

- The larger does may find the process of giving birth to a youngster with a large head easier.

- Lastly, because the BUD has only normal size genes to contribute, you won't find any peanuts in the nest box. (As peanuts have to get a dwarf gene from each parent.)

Lots of breeders use very typy true dwarf does for breeding, just be prepared to find a peanut or two in your litters.

Most successful breeders use both types of doe, the true dwarf and the false dwarf.

There is no evidence to suggest that the larger false dwarfs make the better mothers. The genes that control this factor are inherited completely independently to the size genes, but it is vitally important that you select for this characteristic as well. They are hard enough to breed; the last thing you want is repeated dead litters. So don't breed with does that don't show a strong maternal instinct or with bucks that breed does that are poor mothers. This is one area of breeding dwarfs that divides opinion more than any other. Some breeders will not use the true dwarf does in their breeding programme at all, believing they are too small or typy to breed. Most breeders, us included, use a combination of show standard does and false dwarfs, but we would not use a false dwarf that carries disqualifications. It is important to keep the aim of constant improvement in your mind. The best piece of advice that I could pass on is that breeding does should be selected for the youngsters that they breed, not their show qualities. This is because in the UK adult does are very rarely shown. This is because when judging to the standard adult does cannot compete with the bucks. They are often longer in body and lack the boldness of head.

A major fault that has crept into UK dwarfs in the last few years is the hips that stick out wider than the rest of the body losing the desired parallel body shape required. When the dwarf is turned over the legs are a V shape, not parallel to the body. Whilst this undoubtedly spoils the shape of the exhibition dwarf, there is a far more serious consequence to this feature. Does will often have difficulty breeding as the v shape indicates a narrow pelvis, so the birth canal will not allow the birth of those big headed dwarfs. This feature must be selected against in your breeding programme.

As the does get older their litter size (fecundity) often drops. It is for that reasons that many dwarf breeders don't use does after two breeding seasons. These does are ideal for the newcomer, as they have been kept for a couple of years because they have bred good quality dwarfs. So the new owner should continue to benefit from that, even though the doe will be less prolific.

It is every dwarf breeder's aim to breed a "Pre-potent" buck. This is the buck that no matter which doe he is mated to will produce show quality dwarfs in the litter, and very few, if any, that are pet quality. If you are lucky enough to breed one, it will form the head of your stud for many years to come. We have only had 3 pre-potent bucks in 38 years of breeding and showing. Even if you don't have one, the principles of breeding are the same. In order to increase the desirable characteristics in your stud you have to select which animals to breed together: artificial selection, unlike wild rabbits which demonstrate natural selection. However, as wild rabbits live in colonies of related individuals even natural selection involves the breeding together of these related individuals. This is true of all species in the wild. If you want a good read on the subject, Charles Darwin's "Origin of Species" will take you through the key points of natural and artificial selection. This leads to the concept of "survival of the fittest." In this instance fittest doesn't mean the ability to exercise for longer, it means those are most well suited to their environment are more likely to survive, they will therefore be more likely to breed and pass on those beneficial alleles to the next generation. This is why most wild rabbit are agouti, as this is the best colour for camouflage, so more have survived and passed on the alleles for agouti pattern. Selective breeding has allowed the development of many different colours of dwarfs, indeed many breeds of rabbits and hares. The only possible area of concern is that in the wild when natural selection takes place, there is competition for resources which is essential to allow the survival of those individuals that are better suited to the environment, such as the ability to avoid predators or to thrive on poor quality diet in the winter months. Domestication of all animals reduces the competition for resources and therefore all the offspring don't need to compete so all the healthy offspring survive. The use of specific medication has led to the survival of rabbits that in the past would not have survived. Such individuals should not be used for breeding, remember those alleles will be passed onto the offspring making them vulnerable to the same ailments.

Artificial selection can be a controversial topic and it is thought by some people that related animals shouldn't be bred together. Whilst everyone is entitled to their views, it is often a lack of understanding of genetics and principles of artificial selection. There are various strategies used by rabbit breeders to improve their stock. Often called line breeding, the breeder will mate closely related animals together. Starting with the stud buck or bucks, the most popular method is to keep the daughters from these initial matings and mate them back to their father. Bucks can also be kept but only if they are an improvement on their father. The does from this second generation can be mated back to their grandfather, and so on. Personally I prefer not to mate father to daughter, so the daughters are mated to other closely related bucks and the does from these matings are mated back to the original buck, the grandfather to granddaughter is repeated. This method works for me, and I know of several other breeders who use a similar method. Another popular mating is half brother and half sister. As a newcomer, ask advice from as many people as possible and choose a method that suits you. You must always remember not to mate dwarfs together with the same fault, Of course you can just mate dwarfs together to remove undesirable characteristics and you will breed some really good dwarfs, but in my opinion not consistently. Line breeding had been practised in agriculture for 1000s of years to fix those characteristics such as high milk yield, so next time you pour your milk on your cornflakes think about your next pairings. Whatever strategy you adopt you must practice continual assessment of your stock, looking to eliminate those undesirable characteristics. After several generations of inbreeding you must bring in an outcross, this may be necessary to correct a fault that has crept in, or just to create hybrid vigour. One of the issues related to inbreeding is inbreeding depression, the loss of litter sizes as the animals get more closely related. Introducing fresh genes from different stock will rectify the problem. Lots of exhibitors have different views on when and what type of outcross. The best advice I have ever had on this topic was from the late John Beck. We were having a drink at the NNDRC Adult Stock Show at Halifax, probably about 1985, and he said, the time to outcross is when you are winning, not when you are struggling and after a quick fix. Great advice and we still follow it today. Now, what do you introduce? My advice is a doe which will gradually introduce new genes into your stud. Using a buck, there will be a sudden influx of far too many genes to monitor the effect. Also, we don't use a total outcross, we take a doe from a fellow breeder who has shared stock with us, known as distant outcross mating, so there is a distant genetic link. Mate the doe to your best buck and check the offspring from the outcross carefully, retaining any youngsters that you are happy to add to your breeding programme. It is worth repeating with another buck, again retaining some of the offspring. The exception to the use of a doe, is when your stud lacks overall quality and you need a quick fix. You should look to buy an outstanding buck to head your stud, and then mate your does to him, and continue to line breed back to him.

So after a few generations you will begin to develop a line and your youngsters will be showing more consistency.

Chapter 15

Record Keeping

It goes without saying that accurate records are needed if you are to be successful in building your stud of netherland dwarfs. Following on from the chapter on successful breeding, it is so important that records are kept of what is bred to what and details of the offspring produced in order to selectively breed your dwarfs through many generations to fix those desirable characteristics.

There are many systems available and it is up to the individual to choose the method that works for them. The simplest form is a note on the cage detailing the parents of the inhabitant, which is in stark contrast to the commercial systems available to download onto your laptop, smart phone or tablet. In the USA when exhibition rabbits are sold it is expected that they arrive with a detailed pedigree. This is really easy with computerised system as a pedigree can be produced with a touch of the screen or a click of a mouse.

It is relatively straightforward to set up your own excel spreadsheet to produce an easy to use record system. We currently don't use a computerised system although do keep thinking about taking the plunge. The main reason why we don't is the time involved. Whilst in the shed details of matings, ring numbers of youngsters etc will be recorded, which then need transferring to the computerised system, so I prefer to used a paper based system. I suppose I could just as easily record details straight onto my phone in the shed; call me unusual but it is quite nice to spend time in the shed without the mobile pinging away, I leave it in the house! So for me the back of used prize cards is our method of choice, only red cards of course! It takes two minutes to draw a few lines and add a few details, and then the details of the matings can be added. Any youngsters that are rung are recorded in red so it is easy to see the successful matings. If the doe is swapped to another cage, we just amend the cage number, and of course the does that are the most valuable breeding does have more than one card.

See over page.

17X12345	S.Sable	Sire 11x01610	Dam 16X12345	Cage No. 20
Date due	Mated to	Details		
15.10.17	15X00425	Med. Sable buck. 17X12345 Bold head, ears good substance. Med. Sable buck, lacks depth, pet Smoke doe 17X12346 Bold eye, good colour.		
25.12.17	16X06510	Missed		
12.1.18	16X06510	Dark Sable doe . 18X00304. Excels head for a doe. Med. Sable buck. 18X00303. Good all round Med. Sable doe. Big doe, not rung,retain for breeding.		

In addition, we have a record book that details any dwarf that we have rung in each year, which goes back to our original dwarfs in 1980. The details of each dwarf that is rung is recorded in the book. In addition, as discussed previously, there is a place for the bigger doe in the breeding programme. These does are not rung, as we don't want the ring to become tight, so these are recorded as the same ring number as a litter mate with and A after it, e.g. 18X01256A.

Ring Number	Description	D.O.B	Sire	Dam	Notes
17X00400	S.Sable buck	3.1.18	16X00505	16X00507	
17X00401	S.Sable doe	3.1.18	16X00505	16X00507	Small
17X00402	S.Smoke buck	3.1.18	16X00505	16X00507	
17X00403	S.Sable doe	4.1.18	11x01610	15X00443	Should be a buck it is so nice
17X00403A	S.Sable doe	4.1.18	11x01610	15X00443	Big but good type
e.t.c					

As you can see our record system is based on ring numbers not names. The main reason is that ring numbers cannot be forgotten or changed so there is much less chance of a mistake when recording breeding details. Many breeders use names, again personal preference is the key. As a scientist not only do I use the ring numbers, but also minimal words. Some breeders record when the doe is 5 months and therefore approaching breeding age, I use the D.O.B.

15X00505 Deb's Balule
D.O.B. 10.10.2015
Sire: 11X01610
Dam: 13X10976

The third piece of information is the cage tag. The bucks have the following information.

The does have a little more information; the last two lines obviously changed after each new mating.

16X01876
D.O.B. 15.4.16
Sire: 15X00425
Dam: 14X00467
Mated to 15X00505
Due 12.11.16

When does are mated, I refer to their breeding card which details the results of previous matings, as previously discussed we don't breed father to daughter, so referring to the information prevents that, and as all matings are planned to fit the breeding programme details can be recorded on the breeding card and the cage tag.

As you can see, the doe cards don't have names because we don't name our does, only temporary ones when they won't mate, miss or lose a litter.

We begin to breed our does from approximately 6 months of age, it is often quite difficult to mate maiden does as they often run around the bucks cage which makes them difficult to catch. If the doe hasn't stood for the buck in the first minute, or if she turns on the buck, the doe is held still to allow the buck to mate. If she is still not willing, she is tried again the next day. Remember, matings should be planned so don't try her to any buck just to get her mated, there is no rush. We use younger bucks to maiden does as these energetic young does are difficult to catch, and secondly we are looking to breed young does that will be used for our favoured grandfather to granddaughter mating. We start to use our bucks at about 8 months; maiden bucks are used on an experienced doe, usually a grandmother to grandson mating. What must be remembered is that no matter how much time is spent planning the matings the actual results are the proof of success. If the litter is comprised of just pet quality dwarfs the mating will not be repeated as it is probable that the mating just isn't compatible. The only exception is with a litter of just one, you need more that one youngster to assess compatibility.

An essential item is a calendar; we have one obtained from the National Netherland Dwarf Rabbit Club, which is pre-populated with the dates of the National shows. The most important date is the date of the young stock show, the under 5 month exhibits will be produced from matings 6 months earlier so that is marked on the calendar. Other important dates should also be highlighted, such as important shows. When we started breeding dwarfs in the 1980s once the dwarf reached 5 months it wasn't showable until it developed into a mature dwarf, usually in its second year. The dwarfs of today develop much quicker thanks to selective breeding, so adults can be competitive as early as 7 months. It is at this stage that they are in their best adult coats, so will be more competitive against the other breeds in the challenge. With that in mind breeders are now breeding for the large championship shows such as Bradford and London, mating the does 8 or nine months before the shows, again another reminder on the calendar. For those of us who like our holidays, unless we are lucky enough to have a fellow exhibitor rabbit sitting whilst we are away, it is advisable not to have does due whilst soaking up the sun elsewhere. We cross off the days before the holiday when we don't mate, in our case we don't have does littering within 5 days of us going to make sure any litters are safe in a good nest, and within 5 days of returning to give us chance to clean out and put in a nest box. Of course the calendar on your smart phone can do the job but it is much nicer to look at the stunning photos on the National Dwarf Calendar displayed in your shed.

Chapter 16

The show must go on

For many dwarfites the best part about their hobby is spending time in the shed and trying to breed the perfect dwarf. For others it is showing their dwarfs, but for most people it is both. In the last 30 years the number of shows has fallen dramatically, certainly local shows. When we began showing in the early 80's we could attend Bradford Metro, Leeds Metro, Worth Valley, Doncaster Excelsior, Sheffield, Don and Dearne, Calderdale, Skipton, Knaresborough, York, Bury and Radcliffe, Oldham, Rochdale, Hindley and Leigh, and Blackburn, covering most Saturdays and Sundays in the month. Nowadays many have disappeared or merged together. The demise of these local shows is multifactoral, lack of people wanting to get involved with the running of shows, loss of venues, cost of venues, cost of travel, other hobbies, lack of junior exhibitors, and the list goes on.

What is important is that people must continue to support their local shows, not just exhibiting but getting involved in the running of the shows. Not everyone wants to be secretary, but giving a helping hand to put the pens up before the show or taking them down at the end. A massive step forward is asking exhibitors to remove their own shavings and take them home, saving such a lot of time at the end of the show. The introduction of Vetbed is also proving popular; I personally believe all clubs should be looking to move onto using this.

The ever decreasing number of local clubs is making it more difficult for the National Dwarf club and the affiliated area clubs to find venues to hold their stock shows. The secretaries of these clubs spend a lot of time and effort trying to find venues that are spread around their areas to make them accessible to all exhibitors, so once again please give them your support by exhibiting.

All upcoming shows are advertised in Fur & Feather, so once you have decided which show you are entering the preparation begins. Grooming for the show should be done at home, not when you arrive at the show. On a daily basis your dwarfs should be groomed, running your hands backwards and forward through the coat. Don't forget to check underneath, bucks often become matted in the groin area, especially if used for breeding. This should be groomed out regularly using a nit comb and a slicker grooming brush. This is certainly easier with someone holding the rabbit and blowing into the groin whilst the other groom out the matted fur. Some exhibitors do not use their dwarfs for breeding during the show season; personally I cannot understand the reasoning behind this. The dwarfs are at their fittest during the show season, so if they are in your breeding programme they should be used, not overused. I know of several instances when top *exhibitors* didn't use the buck until retired from showing. How can you line breed back to him for several generations if he is an old dwarf, hence I use the term exhibitor not breeder!

Dwarfs are prone to matting inside their front legs as a result of grooming, the best way to remove this is very gently with a toothbrush. Care must be taken not to pull out the fur leaving the legs bald, unfortunately I see this, and the matted groins, too much when judging. A weak washing up liquid solution rubbed into the knotted fur inside the legs will soften the knots, it is then rinsed off and if this is repeated a few times very little grooming will be required. Check the nails and trim if required, and check the teeth. The judge will do this so it gets the rabbit used to it. Keeping on top of the wet corner will ensure the feet are the correct colour as dirty dwarfs will not win. REW and BEW breeders often have to apply extra treatment to the feet. Washing with the detergent solution may be enough, if not the feet may need bleaching. A common method is to use hydrogen peroxide mixed to a paste using cornflour and applied to the feet. This should be left for a few minutes then washed off. This should not be a regular strategy as repeated treatment will alter the hair structure making it brittle and more absorbent, so the pads lack the density and become even more stained. Posing the rabbit should be done both right and left handed as there are some left handed judges! Also use both hands to pose the rabbit facing you as lots of judges prefer this method of sitting the dwarfs in front of them. Once he is posed step back and admire to assess the overall picture. Unfortunately there are lots of judges who don't do this. What happens if the dwarfs won't stay "in pose"? Just keep trying and hopefully he will begin to settle. Not wishing to be controversial, but I truly believe those that fidget will not have a successful show career. In a big class it is important that your dwarf shows its best features even when not being handled, as the judge will glance at the others when handling the competition for comparison. Don't forget to weigh regularly, again as judges it is really frustrating to disqualify an overweight exhibit, but remember we breed for the correct weight not feed for the correct weight. Once at the show, a quick check over, toothbrush through the front legs, and the groin and in the pen ready for the show. It is advisable to take some shavings (or Vetbed) to the show as in some cases the shavings supplied by the club is minimal. This is a pet hate of mine, there should be enough clean white shavings in the pen. We put a small handful of hay in the pen to give our dwarfs something to nibble during the show, and of course put on the water bottle with water in it. Then it is up to the judge to do their job. In a recent discussion I was surprised to hear what goes through the mind of some exhibitors at the show concerning making rabbits known to the judge. The following were cited as ways to mark the pen and therefore the rabbit: putting extra shavings in the pen, putting hay in the pen, putting distinctive bottles on the pen, using distinctive methods to fasten the bottles to the pen, putting the carrying box under the pen with a name on. Can I say that as a judge I look at the rabbits and not the pen, and as exhibitors we will continue to put hay in the pens and extra shavings (if not enough for the rabbits benefit), put our small coloured drinking bottles on the pen because that is what we bought, use reusable cable ties for our benefit and put our carrying boxes under our pens for our convenience (they don't have our name on).

As mentioned previously, we breed for the National shows as they are the most important shows for us personally and our show season revolves around them. We also attend the area club shows wherever possible, and the big two, Bradford and London Championship shows. The aim of putting all the time and effort into breeding your dwarfs is to compete on the big stage, there is no better feeling than winning Best in Show at a major show.

Chapter 17

Good Health

As with all animals the health is paramount, and the same applies to our exhibition dwarfs. I would argue that the vast majority of show rabbit are much healthier than the enormous numbers of pet rabbits found in the UK. The main reason, I would argue, is the feeding regime. As breeders and exhibitors we feed our dwarfs on the correct amount of high quality feed, compared to a lot of pets which are often overfed on rabbit mixes which encourage selective feeding, the dwarfs picking out the tasty lower fibre elements; in addition they are often given to many high calorie treats leading to many overweight rabbits. In my opinion, feeding the correct quantity of a good quality pellet, with a small amount of oats and unlimited quality hay is the best feed.

Lots of exhibitors have a consistent feeding time, personally I do not feel too strongly about exact timings, remembering that wild rabbits feed at dawn and dusk, we feed hay between 6 and 7am and 2 ounces of pellets/oats between 4 and 8pm. What is important is to observe the rabbits when fed and before the next feed. They should be ready for their evening meal and readily tuck in. Any pellets left from the previous feed could indicate a health problem, but more usually it is a lack of water. Check the water bottle has water and if it has, check the nozzle to make sure it is working. Ours do scale up with lime scale, so we treat with a descaling treatment, taking care to rinse thoroughly.

It is important to check your dwarfs regularly, we check ours weekly when cleaning out, youngsters are handled and checked every day. In all our years of keeping dwarfs we have only taken two to the vets, both valuable breeding/show bucks (valuable in the importance to the stud sense) which had stopped eating and had lost too much condition. Of course with the occurrence of RHD2 (Rabbit Haemorrhagic Disease 2) it is important to vaccinate your dwarfs. I don't intend to go into the biology of viral diseases and the action of vaccinations, that is part of my day job so I'll save it for my A level biology students. Just to say, it is such a virulent disease that we must all be vigilant and vaccinate.

For the inexperienced breeders it is best to seek advice from the more experienced breeders if you suspect anything is wrong with your stock. That is how we all learnt how to alleviate minor health issues. The most common problems are digestive, usually diarrhoea. Often called scours which may progress to enteritis (jelly like poo). Mild forms of diarrhoea are usually easily treatable, the key is to spot it early. The most common cause is a change of food. It is important to try to get some water into the rabbit with a syringe and feed just on hay. A small amount of corn flour or arrowroot made into a paste can also be given. In the past we have fed strawberry leaves if the rabbit will take them. Diarrhoea or scours can also affect newly weaned youngsters due to the stress of taking away from mum. When we wean youngsters we feed them smaller rations of pellets and more hay. When they are with mum each rabbit gets 2 ounces but mum is probably eating more than her share. So once weaned if you give the youngsters 2 ounces each they may gorge themselves, much better for them to fill up on hay. Again water is paramount, syringe some into the affected youngsters. We also feed live yoghurt though a syringe to replace the gut bacteria lost in the faeces. Mild enteritis can be treated in the same way. If the enteritis is really bad, the youngster will be grinding its teeth, hunched up in the corner of the cage and probably not survive the next 24 hours. There are various supplements available that can be added to the drinking water to aid the digestive system, many are advertised in the Fur and Feather magazine. Ask around fellow exhibitors to see if they use any and then the choice is yours.

One condition that is far less common than it was years ago – and I am convinced that it is a change in the treatment – is vent disease. Characteristically this shows up as redness and sores on the vent and often on the lips. Until recently the treatment was a topical antibiotic application to the vent, which was effective at treating the symptoms but not the cause. A far more effective way to treat the cause is injectable antibiotic, usually 3 doses over two weeks.

Head also known as torticollis or wry neck is usually caused by a middle/inner ear infection. If caught early enough treatment is possible using a course of antibiotic injections. There are other causes such as stroke, which don't respond to this course of treatment. Most dwarfs will respond well to the antibiotic treatment and normal posture will be restored after a few weeks. Some dwarfs may not recover fully, resulting in a slight head tilt, but will be quite happy to live a normal life.

Potassium deficiency in rabbits results in your dwarf becoming "floppy" and unable to move. Again, early diagnosis and treatment is the key to a cure. Giving food rich in potassium orally through a syringe may be successful. Tomatoes and bananas are the food of choice, bananas are made into a puree with water and administered, an alternative is tomato puree or even tomato ketchup. As with any condition please seek veterinary advice if the condition persists.

Sneezing is a sound that no fancier wants to hear on the shed but thankfully it is usually no more than a sneeze. Of course the rabbit should be checked to make sure there is no white discharge. Some fanciers will use a cold cure that is designed for humans, just a small amount added to the drinking water. We have never used such a treatment so would not like to comment on the effectiveness. If the sneezing persists a trip to the vets is in order as this could be Snuffles, a highly contagious and fatal disease, therefore the infected rabbit should be destroyed. Any sneezing rabbit should be isolated from the rest of the stock if possible to prevent the spread.

In my opinion the major cause of rabbits being unwell is inadequate ventilation. I have been in so many sheds where there is very little movement of air. The size of the individual cage isn't as important as what is outside the cages. So many people have few, if any, opening windows and then fill all the air spaces in the shed with travelling boxes, storage boxes full of water bottles, food pots, heat lamps. The floor area is covered in a bale of shavings, a bale of hay, grooming table, etc. It is important that adequate ventilation is coupled with lots of free air space. We invested in a new shed in 2014, the shed was designed by ourselves, the major aspect was four opening windows and a stable door with a wire inner door for the top half. The company were surprised that we wanted so many as they automatically put a six inch gap at the top of the walls below the roof. They said this was a recommendation from animal welfare organisations in response to dogs being locked in sheds on hot days with no ventilation. So our shed has a six inch ventilation gap all the way around the top and four opening windows, stable door with wire top, with not too many cages, and lots of free air space. We also have a wall mounted fan that also aids the ventilation. This also helps to remove ammonia fumes from the urine which build up as clean out day approaches. In addition to the unpleasant odour the fumes can cause health issues such as running eyes or respiratory problems. If you already have a shed with inadequate variation all is not lost, a few adjustments to the shed will make a difference, increasing the free air space by de-cluttering is a quick and easy way.

From time to time it wouldn't be unusual for your dwarfs to have what are known as hay mites. They appear as small black flecks in the coat, looking like dust. This is far easier to spot in a white dwarf than a coloured rabbit. They do alter the coat properties, making it feel harsher, losing its ability to roll back. As an exhibitor it is advisable to dust your dwarfs with an over the counter flea powder during the show season. We use Ivomec to remove all internal and external parasites, proving effective against hay mites. Dwarfs that appear to be eating well but not gaining weight to produce that "firm in flesh condition" that is required may need worming. Ivomec is also an effective anti worming treatment, as is Panacur, and there are many other over the counter medications that available from pet shops.

Dwarfs have very thick fur on their feet so do not suffer from sore hocks that are common to rex breeds. There is one exception to this, sore hocks are a sign of poor conformation, the back legs being too long so the dwarf puts too much pressure on its hocks, especially when being posed for showing. There is no effective cure for this condition, the dwarf will not suffer too much with this condition, unless the skin is broken. It is important not to breed with animals with this conformational fault as we are looking for a compact animal with short legs that sits with its back legs flat on the ground.

Along with adequate ventilation, good hygiene is also key to maintaining healthy stock. We clean our dwarfs weekly, removing the wet corners and redistributing the shavings mixed with new clean white shavings. Does that are pregnant often show nesting behaviour that involves starching all the bedding throughout the hutch, hence there is no wet corner. In this case all the bedding is removed when a nest box is added and clean white shavings are added. We use virkon disinfectant sprayed onto the cage floor and walls when cleaning out. This is proven to be effective against many pathogens including RHD2. We wash our food pots regularly and clean drinking bottles at the first sign of discolouration. We have a bottle brush handy at all times and stick to the principle of never refilling dirty bottle. It is important to minimise the occurrence of flies in the shed, good old fashioned fly papers are effective but must be changed regularly. Don't hang them in front of your fan to prevent them drying out too quickly. Good quality UV fly killers are also effective, but there are many cheap ones on the market, you get what you pay for.

It is important that you cut your dwarf's toe nails regularly. It isn't possible to put a time scale on this, regular inspection is the key. Traditionally the nails on an under 5 month exhibit are not trimmed. This is however an unwritten rule, so it should be quite acceptable to do so, but in reality judges would frown upon this, many seeing this as a strategy to disguise the age of your dwarf. Adult dwarfs cannot sit properly with long nails, so a rabbit with long nails is an unhealthy rabbit. As a judge, I see show dwarfs with overgrown nails, and have no choice but to penalise the exhibit as it just cannot sit comfortably. What is also common is for the show bucks to have their pedicures but the breeding animals back home in the shed to be ignored, developing those overgrown nails. Cutting them is straightforward, although now I have to wear reading glasses it is not quite as easy as it used to be. My method is to turn over the dwarf as though judging it, tuck the head under my left arm and cut the 8 nails on the two back feet followed by the 10 on the front feet. It important not to miss the dew claws as if these become really overgrown they may embed into the leg of the dwarf. Care must be taken not to cut into the live blood filled centre of the nail, which is easier to see on a white dwarf, not so easy on a coloured dwarf. Yet another advantage those white breeders have! A good set of nail clippers make life easier and practise makes perfect. Having a firm grip on the rabbit is key, so it feels secure and is less likely to struggle.

Chapter 18

In conclusion.....

Having bred and exhibited dwarfs for 40 years I can honestly say that I get just as excited over the next batch of litters, hoping that there will be that elusive "flier" in the nest as I did in the 1980s, beckoning Deb out to the shed as soon as she comes in from work to see it.

Also, being secretaries of the National Netherland Dwarf Rabbit Club, gives both Deb and I such a buzz, especially the ASS, when the country's best dwarfs line up to be judged. I cannot lie it isn't always plain sailing, especially when it comes to ballot time! However, the pros' outweigh the cons' so here's to the next few years.

For the dwarf fancy to move forward there are a few basic things that must happen:

- Exhibitors must support local shows. The more dwarfs that are shown the more classes will be offered and this will increase the chances of getting specialized dwarf judges.

- Similarly, the area and National dwarf shows need your support, where better to discuss the finer points of our wonderful breed and share opinions of the exhibits being shown.

- Give some thought to joining the committees of these shows, there can never be too many helpers, even if it is putting up a few pens at the start of the shows.

- We must do more to encourage juniors to show, steward and get involved in running shows.

- We must continue to promote the breeder's days and judging seminars, getting more people, including experienced judges to attend. Whilst I agree that the judging of dwarfs is subjective, we do have a standard to judge to. The standard is clearly written, and of late there have been lots of diagrams available to demonstrate the main points of the standard. There is no excuse for the massive inconsistencies that we see in judging, this is clearly not acceptable, and a massive amount of praise must go to the National Netherland Dwarf Rabbit Club for trying to remove these inconsistencies. In any walk of life, training is not only offered, but is compulsory, and people are held accountable for their performance. A premiership football referee has an intensive period of training and then each performance is scrutinized, a poor performance could see them refereeing in the championship. Is it about time that we brought in judges training / CPD and assessment of performance? Exhibitors ask for an honest opinion, but that opinion, however honest, must be based on a knowledge and correct interpretation of the standard, and must not be based on personal preferences.

And finally, I wish you all every success in the breeding and exhibiting of your dwarfs for many years to come, just not too much with your Siamese sables!

Gary Hodson